JOH
KING

D0680079

A WILD LIFE ON EXMOOR

www.r**books**.co.uk

JOHNNY KINGDOM

A WILD LIFE ON EXMOOR

CORGI BOOKS

TRANSWORLD PUBLISHERS
61-63 Uxbridge Road, London W5 5SA
A Random House Group Company
www.rbooks.co.uk

JOHNNY KINGDOM
A WILD LIFE ON EXMOOR
A CORGI BOOK: 9780552154826

First published in Great Britain
in 2006 by Bantam Press
a division of Transworld Publishers
Corgi edition published 2007

Addresses for Random House Group Ltd companies outside the UK
can be found at: www.randomhouse.co.uk
The Random House Group Ltd Reg. No. 954009

The Random House Group Limited supports The Forest Stewardship
Council (FSC), the leading international forest certification organisation.
All our titles that are printed on Greenpeace approved FSC certified paper
carry the FSC logo. Our paper procurement policy can be found at
www.rbooks.co.uk/environment

Typeset in 11.5/16 Fairfield by
Falcon Oast Graphic Art Ltd.

Printed in the UK by CPI Cox & Wyman, Reading, RG1 8EX.

2 4 6 8 10 9 7 5 3 1

To my darling wife

This book is dedicated to you for all the kind things you have done for me and for sticking with me through the rough times. I couldn't have done this on my own. I thought it was the end of the road, after the accident, but you nursed me all the way through. People often walk up to me and say, she needs a gold medal. I'd say she needs more than one. But I must have done something right because if you count our courting days and our marriage, we have been together for forty-seven years. Anyway, darling, it's a big thank you for everything you have done to put me where I am now.

God bless you and our lovely family. Love, Johnny.

Contents

Prologue

When I was a child, my father showed me a rare sight. 'Boy?' he asked. He often called me that. 'Boy, what d'you know about the cuckoo?'

'Not very much.'

'Come on, then, and have a look at this.'

I followed him out and across the front patch of garden and down into the lane. A hedge ran along the other side of this lane and he took a couple of paces up towards the church. 'Look in there,' he said. 'See?'

I peered in and saw a hedge sparrow's nest with one chick in it. But it wasn't a hedge sparrow chick. This one was so big it had literally burst the nest open – the sides had split apart and it sat there, the most ridiculous, oversized-looking thing.

Father said, 'The cuckoo doesn't build her own nest, she lays maybe fourteen eggs, all in different nests, any that she can find. Her chick is born and grows bigger and quicker than the others, and it turfs out any other eggs or chicks it might find in there with it, till it's the only one. Now then, just stand back a pace or two and let's watch.'

We waited, silent and still, for the parent bird to return.

So much of my life has been spent waiting, especially since I picked up a camera. There should be a blank page in this book for every hour I've spent at it. The pages with any writing on them would be few and far between. People don't get to hear about the waiting part, or to see it, but perhaps it's the most important skill to possess. It's brought me the results that I've enjoyed in my career as a photographer of wildlife. The ability to be still, to put myself in the right spot, and wait. I'd ask the reader to remember all the hundreds of blank pages there should be in this book, that we've chosen to leave out.

So there was Father and me, in the lane, waiting.

Eventually the magic part happened: the parent hedge sparrow appeared with a beak full of food, mightily overworked, being a quarter of the size of the monster it was feeding. It flew into the nest – and since there wasn't anywhere for it to land, it perched on top of the cuckoo's back. The cuckoo twisted its head round and opened its beak wide to receive the food. The hedge sparrow could nigh on have walked into that wide-open mouth. You could almost hear the cuckoo saying, 'Come on, get on with it.'

The little hedge sparrow quickly pushed in the food and the cuckoo carelessly gulped it down. The hedge sparrow took off from its back and flew away to fetch more, working like a slave.

It was an extraordinary sight and I've never seen it since. I wish now that I'd had a camera, at that exact moment.

But – none of us knows where life will take us, when we start out.

The beginning

"in early childhood my horizons were
narrow; it was enough excitement to
look for snails in among the cool stones
of the walls, where they went during the
heat of the day . . .**"**

PART ONE

The Beginning

In the village of High Bray, on the southern slopes of Exmoor, there's a patch of waste ground, dead flat, that looks out over the valley of the river Bray. It's a grand view from here: the pattern of fields stitched together with walls and hedges, lines of trees, and the hamlet of Brayford down below, built alongside the river. It's not a view that's changed much in hundreds of years, let alone the sixty-seven that I've known it.

In the middle of this patch of waste ground, among all sorts of other bits of scrap, there rests the carcass of an electric-blue Crystal Maze gambling machine, probably from a pub somewhere. Its innards are torn out and it's lying on its side, abandoned. Bits of broken-down stone-work can be seen here and there, which tell of how the bank was held back, to keep the ground level. It's unused now, but during my childhood this used to be where everyone had their allotments, my father's among them.

A stride or two closer to the village there can be seen, covered with undergrowth, the stumps of old brick buildings, now torn down. These used to be the outside toilets for all the houses. The church looms up to one side, beyond the clumps of laurel where we used to play.

Down through the gate and you come across the village square, on a gentle slope, covered over with tarmac – but underneath are the old cobbles, the slipperiest you ever walked on, which you can still see around the edges. Along the bottom of the square is the same row of old stick sheds, which used to house wood for people's fires. Now they hold bins and suchlike. At the top of the square is an earth bank, which is the boundary of the churchyard. Down each side runs a terrace of houses. On the left, the fronts of the houses open on to the square, whereas, down the right-hand side, it's the backs of the houses; they face out the other way, over the valley. I was born in one of these – the second up on the right-hand side – on 23 February 1939.

A short path with a wicket gate let out on to the lane. Down over, beyond the lane, was the old rectory where Revd Grainger lived – he died young. Beyond the rectory and down the valley a bit, the whole side of the hill was cut away by the quarry where my father worked. It's still there today; the machines are bigger, the hill still moving back, the bluestone taken out and used for roads and building works of all sorts.

Exmoor, with its great slabs of high moorland and its sheltered wooded combes, stretches to north and west and east, all the way to the Bristol Channel, twenty miles away. It would wait for me, but in early childhood my horizons were narrow; it was enough excitement to look for snails in among the cool stones of the walls, where they went during the heat of the day, pulling themselves into their shells to preserve moisture. I peeled them off and set them down on the starting line I'd drawn along the top of a board; then I could watch them race five or six at a time. There was a cricket that lived behind the wall at the back of the fireplace; he made his clicking noise and that's the sound I remember in that house, along with the bells tolling in the church tower, not far off. They rang when there was sad news, like in any village all over the country at that time. The Second World War had started when I was six months old.

My mother, Joyce, was of shortish stature, and round and jolly; she laughed easily. She smoked Player's Weights, a proper grown-up habit, inhaling all the time, breathing the smoke out of her nostrils. Her eyes were blue and her hair curly and black, cut quite short. She wore a pinny while she fed the washing into the mangle. I'd try and turn the handle, to help. It was her work to put the food on the table, turn out clean clothes, keep house for six children and a husband day in, day out, spring, summer, autumn and winter.

My father was named Walter, or more often Bud, but he had better nicknames: the Powder Monkey, the Cat.

He walked to work, his white safety helmet clamped on his head the moment he left the house, his hobnailed boots set one in front of the other, every day for sixty years – out the house, turn right in the lane, up to the church gate, a couple of strides over the bottom corner of the graveyard, down over the bank, across the side of the hill and down the valley a ways ... to Nott's Quarries. He worked with the explosives – hence Powder Monkey. The Cat, because he was surefooted and very fit. To lay charges, he didn't use ladders; he climbed, he leapt from ledge to ledge on the rock face. The Cat never fell. He was so quick, my father. In the pig shed, when the rats became too many, too big and bold to ignore, he'd say to me, 'Boy, lift up those feed trays,' and when I did so, the rats would run up the sides of the door and – *bang* – with his hand he'd have one, and kill it. Sometimes he'd get two at a time. There aren't many terriers so quick as that.

He combed his short wavy hair back over his head. He smoked a pipe, and he had the snuff habit also. He'd take a pinch of Jockey Club snuff from the tin, make a pile of it on the back of his hand, then suck it into either nostril. So his handkerchief turned brown with the stain. The pipe, the Condor flaked tobacco, plus the little snuff tin with the words Jockey Club written on it, all these he put away in the bib pocket at the front of his blue overalls. Round his waist was a broad leather belt with a hefty buckle.

The war was on. Food was scarce. Standing in the middle of the house – I can't remember what I was doing – suddenly two doors slammed at once. This was a freak of nature. An aeroplane had crashed nearby and exploded; the shock wave had run through the house. The silence that followed was eerie. Forces were at work outside of nature that I knew nothing about, but that were close by, that played out over our heads and in the seas not far distant. My father was in a reserved occupation so wasn't called up, but he was in the Home Guard, like many others.

Two Spitfires came down in surrounding fields. I went to see; walking up towards Bentwichen there were pieces of plane stuck in the ground, all over. The other Spitfire came down near Withygate; its tail was sticking out of a crater in the ground. My mother's mother, Granny Moule, brought home a bit of shrapnel which stayed in her house for years. Near Liddicott another type of plane – some kind of bomber or transport plane – crash landed; it tore through three or four hedges before coming to a halt. On the way to see it, at the crossroads, I looked up to see a man swinging in a tree from his parachute straps, dead. When I got to the plane they were towing it away. Someone lifted me into the cockpit. I pretended to fly it while this plane was dragged over the ground, its belly ripped to pieces. I could imagine the man who'd occupied this seat only a short time ago, where I now played. The future of our world depended on all our men and women.

My contribution to the war effort was to make tanks out of used cotton reels. I carved notches in either side for grip, threaded an elastic band through the middle and wound it up with a bit of stick at each end. They crawled slowly, for a short distance. I set them to fight against each other.

German prisoners-of-war were housed in a camp not far away, at Little Bray. They lived in semi-circular galvanized sheds. As the war progressed, they were allowed out to attend our church. They were friendly; they made us toys – monkey sticks and wooden chickens that pecked corn when you pulled the string beneath – and they gave us chewing gum. They worked on the farms, and mixed quite easily. One of them married a local girl.

We made other toys for ourselves. I cut hazel sticks and turned them into whistles. Mother showed us how to dig up clay from the riverbed. We'd carry it home in a bucket and set to work rolling it into little balls in the palms of our hands. She baked them in the oven and we'd paint them in different colours to make marbles. Hollow reeds cut from the hedgerows made good peashooters, with dried peas stolen from the larder for ammunition, or hawthorn berries straight off the tree. Hazel was also used for bows and arrows. Today, I could go to a drawer in my desk and take out a cufflinks box. Inside is a little rusty staple. Before it was in the cufflinks box, this staple was kept safe by my mother. Rewind another few decades and it hung for years on my bedroom wall. Go backwards again, to before we moved house, and there was my mother keeping the staple handy on a shelf so she could tell everyone what had happened. When I was three years old she'd made me a rattle: she'd filled a small tin with nails and staples. It was heavy and made a satisfying sound when I shook it. I went and sat on the front step in the sun and shook it some more, and harder. The lid came off; the nails and staples spilled all over the ground. I must have been curious what these things would taste like. I put a staple in my mouth and swallowed. The first my mother knew of it was the sound of crying. She hurried to investigate and I can remember the high, anxious pitch of her voice: 'What have you done?' I answered her, 'Ate a nail.' The doctor advised waiting forty-eight hours to see if it would appear by itself. If it didn't, well, then they'd have to think of a way to find it. So, we waited. Everyone gave me funny looks. I drank plenty. After two days the staple reappeared; I'd been lucky because it went down the right way, the U-shape first, so it hadn't snagged in my gut. My mother showed everyone the staple. It became a talking point – look what went through John.

So in the blue cufflinks box is part of the toy she

made for me, which travelled right through my gut in 1942. It reminds me of the satisfaction and pleasure gained from toys made by our own hands or the hands of our parents, our uncles and aunts and even those German prisoners.

On Friday nights the galvanized bath was put in front of the fire and we queued up to be washed. There was no mains water supply to any of the houses. The village of High Bray drank, washed and cooked using water from a well dug by my mother's grandfather, a stone-mason called James Moule. The pump is still there, but it is an ornament now; it's no longer used. The water reputedly came from underneath the graveyard and flowed under the death pit where the village's plague victims had been buried in the seventeenth century, before it arrived in the village. Rain would have soaked down through the bones of the past inhabitants, going back hundreds of years, right up to the last grave my father dug, but no one ever got ill.

It was everyone's job in our family to fetch water daily, but on bath nights there were extra trips to the pump so the crock could be put on the fire, the water heated and the bath filled. It was a forty-yard walk across the cobbles. Usually two of us children, myself and either of my older sisters, one each side of the galvanized bucket, walked the water home, where it either stood in the larder under the stairs for the day's use, or filled the bath. During cold snaps the pump and the lead pipe froze, and that would mean carrying water the other way, hot water, to pour in the slot in the top of the pump until it thawed.

In 1947 the snow fell so thickly that we children could stand on the bank and grab hold of the telephone wire. Trenches were dug from the back door of every house in the village – and they led not to cars or to the road like they would today, but to that pump. Fred Friendship, who lived at the end of our row of houses, was quickest to cut his way through. I can see today the lines of these trenches like spokes on a wheel, the people moving along them – almost invisible the snow was so high – to fetch water from the well.

In any case, one way or another we'd fill the bath on Friday night and take our turn. I always went last because more mud stuck to me than to my sisters.

On Saturday nights Mr Thorne turned up in his trilby, smoking his pipe, to collect the rent. It was always paid on time, but there wasn't much money around after Mr Thorne had gone. There was mostly working and keeping going; spending was rare. If my father wasn't walking to the quarry, working a ten-hour shift, and walking back, then he was grave-digging, growing vegetables and fruit, trading moleskins, selling whortle-berries or holly, or poaching for the pot. The Powder Monkey would teach me to work if it was the one thing he did. He and I were the only males among six women, counting all sisters and my mother. He had me on the other end of the double-handed saw, cutting wood. And it was my job to empty the toilet, which stood in a shed up the path next to the vegetable garden. I learned that the bucket didn't fill up so quickly if I used next door's toilet. They had a luxury set-up in their shed: two seats next to each other, a small one for the children and one for the adults. Our shed had only one seat. Squares of newspaper threaded on to a binder cord did for loo paper. It didn't trouble me to sneak into theirs if it meant ours filled that bit slower. But it filled eventually and then it was a Godawful task to upend the seat, grab hold of the handle – yuk – and haul the bucket out, then carry it to the vegetable garden, the wretched stinking thing banging against my leg. There I buried our waste, newspaper and all. It was dug in, and it rotted down to feed my father's prize vegetables. The newspaper cropped up all over, wherever you dug, wherever you planted, reminders of the bits of our family that had melted back into the soil.

Father loved his vegetable garden; it was a passion. He grew a big rack of kidney beans and I was sent down to the railway track to pick up all the old nuts and bolts I could find. These were used as weights to hang off the ends of the most promising specimens and make them grow longer. Father was a showman; he cared about the size of his vegetables and the orderliness of that garden, but a certain amount of corruption in the village had to be sorted out before he could carry off the top prizes. There was a conspiracy among the leading lights at the local flower and veg show. They gave all their best produce to one of their number, so that that person would win. The next year it would be another's turn. Once this web of deceit was untangled, the Powder Monkey saw them off and took the glory for his vegetables which, in a way, we'd all worked so hard to help grow.

Food was important; the war made it so. We trapped our food, shot it, pulled it from the river or out of the ground. We picked whortleberries, or whorts as we called them, on Molland Common or Whitefield Common. My father designed and made a special tool, a set of steel prongs over a tray four or five inches deep, to comb the berries into. He once picked 32 pounds of whorts in one day and sold them to John Brookes' shop in South Molton town square. Or we poached salmon and trout from the river. We were always in the water, in summertime. We'd build a dam to make a pool, a dozen of us or more. My father taught me how to look for trout under the stones, how to tickle them and haul them out with a finger hooked in under the gill. To kill them, it was quickest to put a thumb in their mouths and pull their heads back to break their necks. Then we'd hide them under stones or wrapped in towels in case the bailiffs came by. Or we trapped animals, or shot them. My father was a poacher; it was a task. It answered the question, what shall the eight of us eat today? Among his other work it ranked of equal importance. Except there was one difference: it was illegal.

Here was another source of food: like many we raised a pig in a shed in the garden. It was given household scraps to eat as well as its own food. At the appointed hour Mr Cocksford the pig man turned up and put a rope through the ring in its nose and hauled it up. It hung there, screaming and struggling – a pitiful sight. The sound frayed the nerves. There is nothing like a pig for making you fond of creatures; they have a peculiar intelligence and humour. And when it comes to the end they fight for their lives with every last ounce of strength. Mr Cocksford was sticking pigs on a daily basis, he went around everywhere doing this for folk. He was always accurate: the knife split the artery in its neck. All of us were steeled against the noise. Blood went everywhere and in a few seconds the pig's fighting and screaming slowed, and then stopped. It hung there, dead still, every one of us feeling the sudden silence, the broken-heartedness of death, wherever it occurred, however often. But country folk lived off the land, and they still do; it's their way. The love of animals is bound up with the breeding of them, the keeping of them, their health, the balance of pests and predators, and the killing and eating of them. Animals eat other animals; we are a link in that chain, and always have been.

Pans of boiling water were poured over the pig's skin to scald the hairs. It was my job to scrape them off; I remember that implement, shaped somewhat like a funnel, pointed at one end, which would take the hairs off as you dragged it across the skin. Every part of the pig's body was used. I was given the bladder, tied off and blown up, to use as a football. The carcass was gutted and butchered and put in big round salters and stored in the larder. My dad was a trotter man. Even the head was eaten.

This was the mark of my childhood: the love of animals and yet the killing of them, to eat or to earn money. Turn away from the killing of the pig and go the other way, and there I was, loving my pet mice, spending so much time to make their lives better. It started with the four black and white ones given me by Uncle Bert, my mother's brother. He wore a cap and was wider set than my father and if I remember rightly he worked on the railways. He'd seen the way I loved animals of all sorts and he'd bought the mice from a pet shop in Barnstaple. They arrived in a wire cage. Uncle Bert was handy and had made a box for them to live in. It had a spoked wheel up one end for them to play on; and at the other end was a ramp which went up at 75 degrees to a little balcony affair, which had another little box on it which they used as a bedroom. I loved those mice. I kept them in the washhouse, out of the way, but they lived on me, also. They climbed through my clothes, across the back of my neck, all over my body. One or two lived in my pockets, up my sleeves. Sometimes they came to school with me.

Soon, of course, there were ten mice. And then fifteen. Uncle Bert made another box, with a bigger wheel and two bedrooms. I shifted more stuff off the shelves in the washhouse to make room. More mice arrived and a third box was made, this time with two wheels. It was getting very busy in that washhouse. All three boxes were teeming. At the height of the population explosion I counted seventy mice scampering around in their amusement park. Eventually my dad took to drowning any babies that arrived. I didn't take against him for this, but none the less I wanted to find a way to save them. By this time I was helping with the milking and the shearing and the harvest, and so on, at the farm down the road belonging to Stan and Joan Richards – and I took the mice down there and let them go in the hayricks. It was the best environment for them, I thought, where they could make friends with the wild mice and set up their nests in a warm hay barn. Stan and Joan, and Jim Venn who worked for them, began to notice these odd, black and white mice suddenly appearing alongside the wild ones. They cottoned on to what I was up to but didn't object. In the end I let them all go, some in our pigsty and others down at the Richards' farm. But the construction of those boxes would stay with me, and I'd use the idea again, on a very different occasion, for a different species, many years hence.

Yet it was the same child, myself at eight or nine, who killed moles for money. It was my father who taught me. The trick was also to catch what we called the false moles. Moles are clever, and if you set the trap in their run they'd bore under it and fly the trap with their backs. You'd see your trap had flown, but there was no mole. The 'false mole' was the ghostly name given to these escape artists. However, if you placed a piece of slate either side of the trap, they couldn't bore through that. Instead they went into the trap and were caught.

I made the rounds of my traps – their number increased over the years to nearly a hundred – and I took the moles home. Often Raymond White and I did it together. We walked for miles. And in the very same washroom where I was keeping mice alive and making their lives as good as possible, I was skinning the moles I'd killed. Those mice could have looked out from their bedrooms and from their play wheel and seen me cut through the mole's belly and wriggle my fingers between the skin and the flesh, separating the membranes. I'd work around the back to the spine until the skin came off whole. Then I'd nail the skin to a board; I'd been taught to use four nails but soon learned that six nails kept the skin from shrinking so much. I got some animals too from the rabbit man – fox, badger, stoat. I sent the skins to Horace Friend, a fur dealer who lived up country. I earned anything from a penny to a shilling for each mole skin, depending on its size and condition. If I happened to trap a weasel then I skinned that also. A fox skin fetched five shillings. A badger was like striking gold: two pounds and ten shillings. Badger fur was used for shaving brushes, the fox fur for ladies' wraps, the mole skins for any number of leather goods.

And yet, turn back the other way again, and I hand-reared two baby tawny owls. I was in Parson's Wood when I saw these two little white balls of fluff. They'd fallen out of an old squirrel's drey that their parents had been using as a nest. I carried them home in my hands. It was an emergency, they weren't far off being dead. Mother helped. She showed me how to use a fountain pen to squirt warm, sweet milk into their beaks. Then we moved on to bread and milk. As they grew into larger cages, I trapped mice for them. So while the seventy mice in the washhouse were safe and sound, the mice in Mother's larder weren't. I put traps in the way of their runs, with a piece of cheese on the tiller, and each day I harvested what I'd caught to give to the owls. They regarded me with their mysterious, unblinking eyes, and ate the mice whole, head first. The last thing you'd see was the mouse's tail wriggling into the owl's beak, for all the world as if the mouse were alive and actually scurrying into the owl's mouth on purpose. Later a pellet would appear at the bottom of the cage – the indigestible fur and bones, neatly parcelled up and ejected, the same way it had gone in. When the owls had grown all their feathers, I took them to the big hollow old ash tree up near the church and let them go, but still they came back and pecked at the windows asking to be fed. Mother would say, 'Johnny, your owls is back.' After a while they found their way, and didn't need us any more. They vanished.

More mouths to feed

"Our payment was a couple of rabbits to take home.**"**

My sister Julie was born in 1940, one year after me, and I have lots of memories of she and I doing things together. We were walking once in the road, just a couple of kids mucking about, on the way to Bray Cross. Julie kicked a lump of dung and a tiny little mouse rolled out, fast asleep, just like in a story book. It was a dormouse, hibernating. And a lucky one. It would have dropped off the back of a load of manure and by a stroke of luck it had been discovered; now it wouldn't be run over. Julie picked it up. It had wrapped its gingery bushy tail around itself to keep warm; we put it in the hedge, in a cosy hollow, and covered it with grasses. I hope it lived.

When we were a bit older, around seven or eight, Julie and I plus a whole gang of other kids used to follow the binder. You only see these machines now in agricultural shows, as part of the antique machinery display. It had a cutter on a bed that moved up and down, according to the height you wanted to cut. If there was a lot of weed in the crop you'd want to cut higher; if it was clean you'd set the cutter low to the ground and it might easily scoop up a rabbit or a rat as well. After the corn was cut the knotter tied it into a sheaf and it dropped off the back. In those days the corn grown was oats, mostly. It was our job to follow the binder, pick up the sheaves and stack them in sixes. We'd lean two pairs up against each other, and then one more on each side to make the six. We'd do this for the farmers for no money but we got our reward another way. As the binder went round and round, the rabbits moved into the centre of the field, where the patch of corn grew smaller and smaller with each circuit. As they hid in there, the engine grew louder and closer. You could see the top of the corn moving as the rabbits ran around. At the critical moment we forgot about our sheaves and picked up sticks instead and surrounded the patch of corn. And at the last minute the rabbits made a run for it – this was our chance. We hollered like hell and chased after them. The rabbits bolted every which way, making for the sheaves and hiding in among them or dashing for the edges of the field. Some went 'quat' – they froze, hunched down. In any case, we were at them with our sticks and killed quite a few. However, in the middle of the corn, this time, there was one rabbit hanging on for longer than the others. We could see the corn moving. There wasn't much of an area left to hide in, just a few yards across; soon it would have to make a run for it. We all waited. At last we saw it – not a rabbit but a rat, a full foot long. Up and out he came, and found himself surrounded by all of us. He jumped up and bit Julie on the palm of her hand. Rats have two evil front teeth, yellow and dirty, that they use to gnaw through almost anything, and these teeth hooked into her palm. The rat was hanging off her. She shook her arm like a dog out of water, but it clung on. Raymond White hit it off with a stick. The wound was nasty, as you'd expect. The farmer took her to hospital in his van and she had to stay in there for days with an infected hand.

That mishap aside, the gang of us might take as many as twenty or thirty rabbits to the farmer. He'd paunch them with one swipe of the knife, take their guts out, leaving the liver inside because that was a good part. Our payment was a couple of rabbits to take home.

I wouldn't touch a rabbit now, since myxomatosis, which is a dreadful disease; the creatures loll, slow, spastic, swollen-eyed. It's put me off them, even though the disease is more rare. Back then, though, rabbit was our Sunday lunch, the food we most liked. My mother used to bake them in the oven in a little water. There were hundreds of them. Farms used rabbit men to go round and trap them, just like they used men to catch moles. Their payment was the catch itself, and the farmers would be keeping down numbers. Bill Dockins was the rabbit man in our area, I remember, a shortish fellow who wore a cap, breeches, leggings and even knee pads. He lived near Holewater. I went with him on his round and he taught me how to lay the traps and sieve a layer of fine earth over the top to disguise them. I asked him, 'Bill, what time d'you come round in the morning to see what you got?'

'Six thirty.'

'All right, see you then.'

So I went round the traps half an hour earlier, at six, and sneaked a couple of his rabbits. I'd learned that sometimes they pulled themselves free, or even gnawed their own foot off, so they could escape. So I'd leave just a little bit of the paw in the trap so it looked like it had got free. That way he'd be none the wiser. And that was two rabbits for the pot – Sunday lunch.

When my sister Julie arrived in our household there were three of us in the bedroom, myself and two sisters. We were beginning to crowd each other out. In 1945, when I was around six, the opportunity came up to rent the house next door, number one, which stood at the end of the terrace, on the corner, and had three bedrooms. It was much the same downstairs, one room plus a larder with a Bodley fireplace and lino covering the stone floor – except the room was wider across. The table was bigger and so the forms or benches alongside could take more backsides. There would be eight of us eventually round this table: my mother and five sisters, Father and myself. The garden was better too. I had my own bedroom because I was a boy, meanwhile the girls – five of them eventually – shared the second bedroom, and my parents had the third.

I was restless at night. Never mind that I was actually asleep, I got up and walked all over that house. My father followed me out of the bedroom, downstairs to the larder, where I picked up a cup of water and drank it – sound asleep the whole way. He saw me crash head first off the bed on to the floor, while I dreamed that I was diving into the river. In the dead of night he walked in to find me kneeling by the side of the bed with my arm under the pillow, fingers wiggling. In my dream, the pillow was a stone in the river and I was tickling trout. He once ran into the bedroom and caught hold of my leg just as I was crawling out the window. God knows where I thought I was going; probably I dreamed I was stealing eggs from a nest, or climbing a cliff, or maybe I was playing fox and stags. It was a favourite game of ours – all the kids in the village would take part. I was often the stag because I had a talent for running away. The others would give me a half-hour start. I'd run – down to the bridge, up the river, through thickets and climbing over fallen trees, up past Little Bray, over the top of the hill. By now they'd be after me, calling like a pack of hounds. I'd run down the hill towards Broomhill. They'd cut corners, head me off. Once they trapped me down by the garages there and I climbed up and ran across the roofs, jumping from one garage to the next while they bayed for my blood below. On my next jump I went clean through the asbestos roof and fell on top of an Austin 7 car parked inside. All hell let loose. Mr Dennage came out and grabbed us all, threatened us with the police. Who was going to pay for the damage to the garage and to the roof of his car? In the end all the parents clubbed together to pay him back.

So maybe, that night, I dreamed I was the fox again as I crawled through the bedroom window. The fall to the ground below yawned beneath me. My open eyes were blind; I was fast asleep. Father rushed over and grabbed my ankles and pulled me back. I knew nothing about it; I remained asleep despite his shout. He swivelled me round and pointed me back to the bed and I fell between the sheets, still mumbling and muttering.

Right there and then, Father went round all the upstairs windows and tied them shut with bootlaces.

These weren't anxiety dreams; it wasn't the behaviour of a troubled or conflicted child. It was only that, at night, I relived what had happened during the day. Every morning I awoke none the worse and went down and ate a slice of bread and syrup. I still have that slice of bread and syrup, first thing.

As I've come to write this book I've realized how strong an influence on me was my father. It wasn't always good between us, by any means. He wasn't above giving me a leathering with that belt he wore around his overalls; we had fights and arguments at times. I probably had a better relationship with my mother; we had fewer fights for sure. I was a bit of a mother's boy, to be honest, although you wouldn't think it, the amount of things my father and I did together. But I'd follow my mother around just as much. She was always busy. On Mondays it was washing day. I'd help with fetching sticks for the furnace, to heat the water. The scrubbing board would come out. Washing took real elbow work. Then the clothes would be rinsed. A blue-bag would be added, to help the whites come out better. Then it was the mangle, and you had to watch your fingers because the rollers were heavy. The clothes were then hung out to dry. Washing took the whole of Monday. On Tuesdays, it was ironing. Mother had two flat irons, one heating on the Bodley stove while she used the other. Come the time to swap around, she'd test for temperature by lifting the flat iron off the stove and spitting on it. You needed a good sizzling sound for it to work.

She was in the Mothers' Union, and took part in church life. She had her own windowsill in there, which it was her task to keep up with flowers. During her birthday month, May, she'd do the flowers on the altar too. I was also involved in the church – I sang in the choir, I went to Sunday School, and I still have the books we were given, one each year. I watched Mother do the football pools and if the Brayford football team were playing at home she'd go and watch them, including her own husband playing in hobnailed boots – you'd know about it if he caught you in a tackle.

Saturday was baking day. She made an egg tart that couldn't be bettered. Sunday afternoons were for darning. Any or all of these days, I was close to her.

But it was Father who gave me everything, in terms of what I was most interested in, what I ended up doing, and working at. He had the same love of animals as I did; he was up to his elbows in the life and death of creatures, just like me. He was my teacher as well as my parent. And I was learning fast – with the poaching, and by keeping pets of my own, and by observing creatures in the wild. I think it's true that most people don't notice wildlife even if it's right under their noses, but only because they're not as interested as I am, and as I have been all my life. It's like exercising a muscle – the more you look, the stronger you are at seeing.

It was learning, yes, but not the sort you can get in a classroom.

I went to school, of course, but the teachers weren't always best pleased to have me there. I swore a lot, I played truant, I answered back. I was out to make my friends and

classmates laugh; that was the whole point of school for me – and good fun it was too, at times. But it didn't suit the teachers, that was for sure. Mrs Bond was our head-mistress. She was a good woman. I always liked Mrs Bond. I still know her today; she's built a smart white house that stands on the exact same spot, incidentally, where I fell into a pit of human muck, which sorry tale I'll be telling later. She's in her eighties as I write this, so she must have been a young headmistress back then. I remember she took us on a nature walk; we were a couple of loops of the river upstream from the bridge at Brayford. The river Bray was by this time my playground. I knew its banks, its pits and waterfalls, its currents, like the back of my hand, winter or summer. We came to a crossing, a series of stepping stones. I wanted to impress Mrs Bond. I called to her from my stone, 'Should I catch you a trout, Mrs Bond?'

'Oh yes, go on, then,' she said, laughing. 'Catch me a trout.'

She thought I was joking.

I knelt down and slid my hand in the water. A flight of shadows over the bottom of the river had already told me the fish had made for safety, hiding among the weeds and under stones. This was summer and the water was warm enough; no one who tickles trout likes cold water because it gives you white-finger, one of the maladies of the profession – fingers numb with cold and white as paint, bloodless. I moved very slowly, reached down under the stone. There was a trout there; I felt its side, slippery as oil. I was lucky to find one of a proper size; I guessed it was half a pound or so. It lurked under this stone while I played my hands along its belly and sides. I've always wondered what on earth a trout thinks is happening, but of course it's not thinking, as we understand it. It's a form of hypnotism, I suppose. The difficult part is to lift it out of the water, especially if it's small. They're more slippery than a bar of soap – one twist and they're gone. I slipped a finger into its gill and pulled it from the water. It was hooked; couldn't escape. I stood on my stone in the middle of the river and held it up.

Mrs Bond was stepping daintily across, some way behind.

'Mrs Bond, I got you one!' I cried. She almost fell in. Her hands flew to her mouth when she saw it, as it hung there, flapping and scattering water.

'Oh, dear me!' she exclaimed in her educated voice, 'What are you doing? What have you done? You put that back in the river, right away!'

My face fell. I didn't understand why she was cross. Didn't she want to eat it?

There were other teachers whom I liked and got on well with. Mrs Bowring, for instance. But there were some I didn't like. Mrs Cobley had an authoritarian streak which didn't sit comfortably with me. For instance, I was naturally left-handed, but she tied my left hand behind my back to force me to use the right one. My sister Julie crept up behind my desk and untied me, but Mrs Cobley wasn't put off. She tied the knot tighter. Julie came up again, and still managed to untie the knot. And so it went on. I swore a lot. There was another boy who was worse. She took us out and washed our mouths with soap. There was one boy, who shall remain nameless, who pushed Mrs Cobley into her own store cupboard and locked the door. The class all ran off. Mrs Cobley was rescued by someone at some point, obviously, because she was back to work the next day, none the worse but with a bigger frown on her face than ever.

One Monday morning two police officers came to the school and asked to speak to myself and David White and Brian Southcott. They told the three of us, in no uncertain terms, that someone had seen us the previous day. We'd already had a roasting from our families, but now we were going to be charged with trespass and malicious damage, maybe.

They separated us from our classmates and took us into the other school room. Their faces were stern and uncompromising. We knew exactly why they were here. David still had the bruises and scratches. I still had the headache.

'So,' they said, 'what were youse about?'

The previous afternoon – a Sunday – the three of us had gone out looking for birds' eggs. It's not something that should be done nowadays, but back then it was a regular practice for boys of our age to clamber up and down the cliffs near Lynton, say, in the Valley of Rocks, and collect gulls' eggs. We'd carry them back in a wicker basket and sell them to the hotels for a penny a time. If there was one egg in the nest you'd leave it so as not to discourage the parents. If there were two eggs, you took one. If there were three or more eggs, you left the nest alone because it meant they'd probably begun sitting and, likely as not, the foetus inside the egg would have begun to form.

On this Sunday, we weren't on the cliffs, we were inland, close to where we lived. It was a hot summer's afternoon and in these conditions the high moor can feel like a desert. We were happy to walk in this combe, cooler in the shade of the trees and with the river nearby to drink from. As we made our way upstream, walking along a rough cart track, we glimpsed a roof through the trees; then we made out the house itself. It was a cottage, tucked away in this remote spot. We thought nothing much about it until, as we drew closer, a host of birds, jackdaws mostly, suddenly scattered from the top windows of the house, from the chimneys, from the eaves, like in some horror story. We watched, surprised at the number of them, and the fact they'd come from out the windows. It could only mean the house was deserted.

And of course, where there are birds, there are eggs.

The jackdaw is easily identified by its striking plumage and its greyish head. It lays a blue egg with black spots. It's an attractive egg to look at, to hold in your hand.

We came to the house – called Osbeer Cottage. The top-floor windows were broken in places. The garden was overgrown. The heat shimmered off the snaggle-toothed slates in the roof. We went closer and called out. There was an eerie silence – no one around. The birds watched us from the surrounding trees, alarmed. We wandered in the garden for a while. How could we get to all those eggs? There were dozens of nests up there, tempting us.

We scouted around the house, tugging at the windows and doors. They were nailed shut. We searched for an old ladder that might have been lying around, but found nothing. Eventually we reasoned that it wouldn't be a crime to break a downstairs window, since so many on the top floor were already gone anyway. We burst the glass with stones and crawled into the house. We found ourselves in a shadowy, dark interior, the floor covered in dust and sticks and fragments of plaster. The odd piece of furniture lurked at the edges of the rooms, practically invisible, coated in the same dust as the floor. We felt our nerves tingle; it was a ghostly experience to be in here, where we weren't meant to be.

We weren't interested in exploring downstairs; we

were after those blue eggs with black spots. We found the stairs and climbed, our footsteps printing in the dust, trails left by our hands on the banisters. Upstairs, the dilapidation and abandonment were more obvious. The birds had had free rein up here for a while. Feathers, droppings and debris from nest-building littered the floors. The weather had got in and was rotting the wood-work, so it smelled of damp. We walked from room to room, looking for nests. We didn't find any, but we could tell where they were. In each bedroom there was a fire-place and the amount of detritus in the grate and on the surrounding hearth showed that the nests were in the chimneys. David said he was going up to find one.

He went and stood in the fireplace, peering upwards. Brian and I told him not to be daft; he'd only get stuck. David found a foothold and hauled himself up one step. 'Don't do it,' we warned him. He stepped back down and joined us. 'I'll be all right,' he said, 'if I take my clothes off. There's enough room.' He pulled off his shirt and dropped his trousers and stood there in his boots and underpants, thin and white in the gloomy old bedroom. 'I'll get up there,' he repeated. We could only believe him.

He started climbing. We watched as his legs dis-appeared. We could hear his scrabbling behind the chimney breast. It sounded like a wild animal. Plaster and small stones fell into the fireplace, dislodged as he squeezed up. Brian and I stood there staring at the wall, our gaze inching higher and higher, following the sound. We kept on calling to ask if he was all right.

After a while the scrabbling stopped. There came a muffled word or two. 'What?' we called. There was more scrabbling and then silence again. 'You found one?' we asked. There came the sound of more struggling, a grunt.

'You all right?' we shouted.

'I'm stuck,' came the muffled answer.

I reached up and grabbed hold of his ankles and tried to tug him down. It didn't work. He was jammed in the chimney. Brian and I looked at each other. Exactly what we'd feared would happen, had gone and happened. We shouted advice up to him: to take his feet clean away from the sides, to try and twist round, unscrew himself downwards.

We were worried now. We had to get him out of there somehow – and we didn't want to run for help because we weren't supposed to be here, we'd broken in.

Brian and I hauled at the bedroom fireplace to see if we could get it out but it was screwed tight to the wall. We ran downstairs and searched for something to use. And then we had a stroke of luck: we found a pickaxe. It wasn't long before we had the fireplace away from the wall. Then we set to work knocking the stones out. Over and over we beat against that wall with the sharp point of the pick. When one of us grew tired, the other took over. Piece by piece the chimney breast came down. We could see a pair of legs, David's middle . . . and suddenly he dropped out of the chimney, black as the ace of spades from all the soot: it covered him from head to toe, except for the whites of his eyes. We picked him up and wiped him down, him swearing all the time at the good luck, having escaped. He quickly got dressed; we all felt the devil at our backs as we ran from the house, climbing out the same way we'd come in.

Once we were in the garden we could stop and catch our breath. We were none of us the worse for wear. No one had seen. We were safe.

We lay down in the hot sun and thanked our lucky stars. The long straggly grass was dry and comfortable under our backs.

The jackdaws wheeled and flapped overhead. Before long, we went back to our original question – how could we reach their nests? There was one sitting on top of a drainpipe: a big untidy clump of twigs. You could see how the pipe had become blocked and rainwater stained the wall. Being an old house, it was an iron pipe, screwed into stone, so when I gave it a good pull it held firm. I could climb up and reach the jackdaw's nest, no trouble. I'd inherited my ability to climb from my father. An iron drainpipe was easy.

I made a start, hauling against the pipe to keep my feet glued to the wall. As I went 10, 15 feet up I pulled harder still, because it was getting high enough that if I fell I'd hurt myself.

Just as I was reaching the top, three things happened almost in the same instant. First, the top bracket unplugged from the wall and the drainpipe came away; it was nothing less than a heavy iron bar falling through the air. If it came down on top of me I'd be killed or seriously hurt. Second, the nest was dislodged from the top and came raining down in a shower of sticks and feathers and speckled blue eggs. Third, I fell to the ground with a tremendous *whump*, landing face down. It knocked all the wind from me. When I came to my senses I didn't know what day of the week it was.

The second piece of luck we enjoyed that day was that the iron drainpipe didn't land on top of me. I was winded and took a while to recover, but I was unhurt.

Suddenly we realized how long we'd been away – hours. And we were far from home. We set off quick; it was getting dark even as we ran. We knew we were in trouble, without question. Sure enough, when we eventually arrived home our families were worried to death. My mother was grateful to see me back but Father's temper was up. The belt came off. I'd felt that heavy buckle across my backside before and I would again, more than a few times. I took my punishment and went to bed, smarting, but at least I was alive and back home.

The next day we were all just about picking ourselves up from that adventure and looking to find a new one when those two police officers caught up with us at school. It was frightening to face up to them, but they only gave us a verbal warning; no charges were brought.

Someone must have seen us coming away from that house. I often wonder who it was, and what they saw.

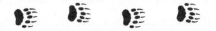

In time my father would apprentice me into all his professions: I'd be a poacher just like him; I'd work in Nott's Quarries as he did; and I'd be a gravedigger all my life.

In these early years I was still too young to help with the gravedigging, as I would when I reached twelve or so, but I went along to watch, and on dark winter evenings I held the tilley lamp and moved from spot to spot around the edge of the grave so that they could see where they were digging. Father was helped, at that time, by Derek Sharp, who would later become my brother-in-law.

The church loomed in the darkness. The old graves stood crookedly, round about, tablets of stone with words of love and remembrance written to those who'd passed away. The long-time dead, of course, were continually being dug up. You can't have a churchyard as old as that and keep on burying your dead there without disturbing ground that's been used over and over before.

The two of them worked hard, breaking up the earth with the pick and spade, throwing it out with the shovel. It took two and a half to three hours to dig a grave, if the earth was soft and the weather was fair. They went lower and lower until just their heads were visible above ground level. A decent grave is six feet deep. As they went down I saw complete skulls, teeth, leg bones turned up by their forks and spades. I rubbed the earth from the brass handles of coffins, all that was left after countless years in the earth had rotted the wood to nothing.

Once, with a grunt and a snap upwards of its prongs, my father lifted a complete skull on his fork. It jerked into the glare of the tilley lamp like in a horror film. Father gave a loud shout, 'Christ!' That shout, and the sight of this ghoulish white mask, suddenly alive in the glare of the lamp, sent alarm right through me, scared me to death. I dropped the lamp and took off, scattering in all directions. After a twist or two I got my bearings and headed for home. It wasn't far – down through the church gate, along the lane a hundred yards, across the front patch of garden and I was there. Every step of the way it was as if that skull, chased me. I banged into the house and headed straight for the safety of Mother's arms. It was all I could do to get the words out quick enough, to say what had happened, how the head had been stuck on Father's fork, he'd lifted it out of the grave . . .

Many, many years hence, I would be in that very same churchyard, spending those same two or three hours – quite senior in years myself – breaking up the earth with pick and spade, lifting it out with the shovel, digging with my own hands my father's grave.

In 1950, aged eleven, I changed schools. I went to the South Molton Secondary, on the corner of North Street. Suddenly there were an awful lot more people and half a dozen teachers. The whole pace of life shifted up a gear. I started on a lifetime hobby: chasing girls and looking for mischief, and being as wild as I could get away with.

There was one girl called Julie Mayne who was ever so pretty, and an added attraction was that her parents ran the pub where the poachers went. She was practising netball when I started out chasing her. She ran clear across the court and I went after her. There was a blue door leading into a shed and she ran in there to escape. I dived in and quick as a flash shut the door behind us. Maybe I could get to kiss her. There was a skirmish in the shed between us. Pretty quickly she tried to run away again, and that's when we found that the door wouldn't open. It was a Yale lock; we were trapped. That suited me – she couldn't escape. The other kids outside started shouting, 'Johnny Kingdom's locked in the shed, he's locked in the shed with a bit of stuff!' I can see right now how pretty she was and I knew how all the poachers looked at her; this was my turn. It took some time before they found the key and came to unlock the door. Witnesses were called. It was my fault – I'd done it. Julie and I were taken to the headmaster, Mr Hawkes. The walk to his office was horrible. I knew what was at the other end of it. The writing down of the crime in the punishment book. Then Mr Hawkes, handing me the cane, slim and with plenty of whip to it, with a knob at the top; I came to know it well. The carrying of the cane back to the form master. Leaning over the desk and listening out for the *whoosh* and then the burning, harsh pain. I put my hands on my backside to protect it, but all that meant was that my hands were hit and that was even more painful. What was wrong with chasing a girl into a shed, for darned hell's sake? As far as I'm concerned there's something up if boys don't chase girls into sheds. It's only looking for a mate, which all creatures do, from the minute they're big enough to lift a foot over a piece of straw.

Within twelve months we were all moved en masse to a brand-new school building, which had been built on the southern edge of the town. It was bigger again, and better, with prettier girls to chase and long corridors to chase them down. It was a different store cupboard, but it was still me and a girl in it, me trying to kiss a girl too old and too big for me. Mrs Franson, the science teacher, caught me this time and I was sent again to Mr Hawkes, the headmaster. I was written in the punishment book, just the same, and I walked the same walk back to the class, carrying the same cane as had been brought from the last school. The difference was, this time, I was beaten in front of the whole class. Mrs Franson made me lean over a desk, and the others all sat and watched as she hit me across the backside as hard as any man would have done.

Just the other day I bumped into Julie Mayne in the street in South Molton. She's nearly seventy now. I shouted to her, 'I can see you in your green knickers, Julie!' the same as I do every time I see her. It still makes her laugh. Those green knickers were real passion-blasters, mind. If you were courting it would take a lot of hard work to get through all that elastic. It was Julie – and the other members of the netball team – whom I was trying to impress when I turned from watering the garden and stuck the hose between my legs and pretended I was watering the plants myself, not with water. The headmaster looked out the window and saw me straying from the task I'd been set and there I was again – the cane came out.

Mr Cross taught agricultural studies and took us out naming trees. He told me, 'Johnny, hop up into this hedge a minute.' I did as I was told. He handed me a knife. 'Now choose one of those hazel sticks growing there.'

'This one, Mr Cross?'

'That'll do. Now cut it down for me, would you?'

'Very good, sir.' I cut the stick.

'Now fetch it down to me.'

I jumped off the hedge and handed it to him. 'There you go, sir.'

'Thank you. Now bend over.' He took the stick and gave me six of the best across the bloody arse with it. 'Now! You won't swear again,' he said. 'Hmmm?'

'BLUDDY HELL, Mr Cross, I'll stop swearing if you stop bluddy beating me,' I shouted.

I've never stopped swearing, not ever.

It was Mr Cross who hit me across the knuckles with a ruler when it wasn't my fault. It had been a bad year for fruit and there were only two apples on the apple tree in the school grounds, and one of them had disappeared. I hadn't taken that apple, but I got the blame for it. I don't know why. The person who had stolen the apple, I believe, watched the ruler come down across my knuckles and took fright, because not long afterwards the apple was replaced. Believe it or not, it was pinned to the very stalk that it had been taken from, and hung there large as life. I still think about that person. Who was it that saw me take the punishment for it, and then went to such lengths as to *pin the apple back on the stalk*? One very guilty person, whoever it was.

I wasn't academic. I was only good for three things at school: getting into trouble – that was my number-one achievement – and sport, and art. I could faithfully copy pictures of birds and animals, so Mr Stewart, the art teacher, was a man I got on with. I once did another boy's art exam for him and he came first and I came second. You might say I swept the board on that occasion.

Percy Banham was a general teacher, but he was our sports master as well. He was a good man. He liked me. I see him very often these days, with his wife, when we have Sunday lunch at the Coaching Inn. He saw the point in a boy who wasn't good at academic subjects. I was very fit and good at cross-country. I won it outright two years running, and myself and Doug Harris were invited to run with the North Devon schoolboys, competing against teams from around the country.

Yes, running away – that was something I'd need to be good at.

It was the way Father carried himself, the light in his eye – I could tell something was going to happen.

About four days beforehand, he told me what it was. Would I like to come with him and a gang of other men and go out poaching, at night, with the lamp? That wound me to a fair old pitch of excitement. All my poaching to that date had been done under cover of daytime, so to speak. This was a step up, like a graduation. And a test. I was invited into the world of grown men.

That evening I watched as Father took out this huge lamp to clean it and check it over. It was a massive round globe of a thing, near enough twice as big as a football, and heavy. Inside, when you swung open the glass front, were three mantles, equally spaced out in front of a curved mirror. It was those mantles that would burn and kick out the watts. A hand pump pressurized the fuel so it would vaporize and glow with white heat in each mantle. It was an awesome piece of equipment.

My father, during the day's work at the quarry, had had a quiet word with seven or eight men – the usual suspects. It was a simple message, one they were quite used to hearing: six thirty, Friday night, meet by the bridge? A simple nod in return. They'd be there. I was old enough, he told them. In fact, as it turned out, there would be another boy there, younger than me.

It was November. The salmon would be running upstream.

I could hardly wait. School dragged by. I sleepwalked and talked around the house. I couldn't concentrate and thought only of what was coming at the end of the week.

Eating and sleeping were like chores, just in the way.

At last the hour arrived. It was pitch black outside the house. I pulled on welly boots, warm, dark clothing; Father the same. He fetched out the gaffe from where it was hidden in the cupboard. A gaffe is a metal hook attached to a stick, with a length of rope connecting the two. It's a professional piece of equipment, unlike the dung fork used by old Bill Niven. I'd been surprised at him, a chapel man – good and righteous, he was – forking salmon out of the river. 'Leave the salmon alone!' he'd always sternly tell us, and no wonder, I thought, when I saw him, bold as brass, carrying a West of England grain sack, blood dripping out of the bottom of it, leaving a trail behind him. Yes, he wanted us to leave the salmon alone, all right – so he could take them for himself. I followed him once and found out what he was up to. He took his dung fork up the track beyond the mill, to where the fender came down and stopped the water. He put the fender down and watched the water drain away. Then he skipped around in the riverbed, forking up the salmon that flapped about, stranded. This was out of season, mind, so even though he owned both the mill and that stretch of the river, it was illegal, it was poaching. Thanks for the lesson, I thought, and it wasn't long before I was copying him. Except I had to be double quick so that he didn't notice, sitting in his mill, that his wheel was slowing down, that the water had stopped flowing.

Anyway, this Friday night, Father took out the big mantle light which I'd watched him clean and check over earlier in the week. He pumped the handle which pressurized the fuel; it was a vigorous action that took some minutes. When he turned the valve it hissed loudly – it sounded dangerous. Added to the winter darkness which closed in round the whole village now, and the fact we were going out, at night, to trespass and to steal as much salmon as we could lay hands on, it was no wonder I was afraid and excited. Father took the lighter out of his bib pocket on the front of his overalls, struck a flame and lit the mantles one by one.

It kicked out a brilliant white light, too intense to look at directly. It was something like a car headlight, but with a broader throw. As we stepped out the back of the house and walked across the square, anyone in the houses around could see us and know what we were up to, couldn't they? Why else would the Kingdoms, father and son, be out at night carrying such a great big light? I felt we were taking an unnecessary risk. Surely we should have waited until we were out of sight, upstream? The light showed up all the houses, every window. Father told me not to worry. As far as he was concerned the village was on our side and people would keep their mouths shut.

We walked down over the field towards Brayford, just a

mile away. The lamp would have been seen from miles around. Bailiffs all over the county would have been picking up their cudgels from their front doors, heading our way. The light flooded the fields ahead of us, sloping away from the village, the illumination just as strong as that given off by the bonfire on Guy Fawkes night just a week earlier. Us children had been in charge of getting together all the rubbish, collecting everything from the leavings of the storms in the roads – old branches and so forth – plus everyone's combustible scrap. When it came to building the bonfire, we'd put an old tyre in the middle and fill it with waste oil, just so it started easily. We strung a rope around the fire for safety's sake but there were accidents over the years – young Bill Yeo was badly burned when someone lit a Roman candle and put it in his front pocket – but the whole village came up to watch and there were sausages, and so on – a party for the whole village. And it was such a pleasure to see the firelight carry over the fields into the valley below. There was that sense of being a beacon that could be seen for miles. I had the same sense tonight, but it gave me a different feeling: I felt very conspicuous. Anxiously I looked as far as I could, at the edges of the light, to see if anyone was going to appear and stop us. No one did.

At Brayford, right on the bridge, we met the other four men, so now there were seven in all, including myself, nearly fourteen at the time, and another boy.

Where it was dark the river was black and moved like oil, but where the light shone on it you could see every stone and scrap of weed on the riverbed. The overhanging trees were either ghostly black fingers against a dark sky, or brilliantly lit and seeming to sway as the lamp swung back and forth.

We started to walk upstream. All the way up, pairs of salmon would be busy at their 'work', as we called it – laying their eggs. They fight their way up from the sea, a journey of many long miles, moving through water that's often too shallow, leaping up waterfalls, wriggling through rapids, uphill all the way. When they reach the pool they themselves were born in, they stop. They move over what we called the stickles, the shallow bit of the pool behind the main pit. The female salmon is called the sow; the male is known as the keeper, and he can be identified by the hook on his mouth. Both keeper and sow work together to dig the hole for the eggs by fanning their tails over the sandy bottom. When they judge it's deep enough the keeper moves to one side and the sow positions herself over the hole and lays her eggs. As soon as she's done, you will see the keeper push her aside and cover the eggs with his milt to fertilize them. Then they both move forwards one length and use their tails again to backfill the hole and cover the eggs. Finally, they move two or three pebbles over the spot, to prevent other salmon disturbing their eggs. Then they're done; the job's over. At this point they've become what we call 'spent out'. The pallid, tasteless flesh of the spent-out salmon is the proof of how dearly it has cost them. It's been an enormous effort. They've worked tirelessly for as long as a month. During the journey upstream they won't have eaten. They've maybe lost a third of their bodyweight. Now they've laid their eggs, they give up the ghost. They allow themselves to be carried back down to the sea, but only if they're lucky will they reach it. Many die along the way. It's a touching thing to witness the breeding of salmon every year, the way they work together – and work so hard – to find their way back to the same spot where they were born.

The trick is to catch them before they're spent out.

We stopped at the Whirlpool, as it was called, just under Little Bray. It was a pit around seven feet deep, on a sharp bend. We moved as silently as possible up to the bank, watching the pool of light as it moved over the water, not in the deeps but at the back of the pool, over the stickles. The salmon, waiting there in pairs, showed up as white streaks. Father held the light so it fell just a foot to the near side of the salmon. They moved towards the light, like moths. He moved the light another foot, steadily, slowly, drawing them towards the bank. Sure enough, the salmon drifted into the light. A third time he moved, and they followed.

After some minutes the salmon were lying right

alongside. Quietly, smoothly, the gaffe was inserted, which broke the surface of the water just above the salmon. The hook went into the belly of a salmon and it was lifted smoothly, quickly, on to the bank, flapping around. The rest of us were on it. One clout on the back of its head with a stone killed it instantly. We used the usual West of England sack to put the catch in. To begin with I was charged with carrying it. When we'd finished at the Whirlpool I wound the top of the sack and hauled it over my shoulder – 10 pounds of weight. One salmon caught, but the river was full of them. We were off our knees and walking upstream to find the next one. Father pumped more pressure into the lamp and then carried on ahead, lighting our way.

Now that we were alongside the river, I didn't think about being caught by the bailiffs. No houses overlooked this part of the valley. The light was on the water itself. The trees and the undergrowth and the depth of valley shrouded us.

This was our work: to catch salmon for our tables or for sale. It was illegal, we knew that well enough, but there was no sense in us that what we were doing was wrong. We were hungry, we killed for the pot, for the table or for other people's tables. We viewed the bounty of the river and the land as wild, and therefore the right of any man or woman to catch and eat. In our eyes it was those who claimed ownership of wild animals who were in the wrong.

I'm not sure I would say any different now, but I've not poached for many years.

We worked our way up as far as Leworthy Bridge. By now there were ten or eleven salmon in the bag – one of 16 pounds – and it was around eleven o'clock. Everyone was well satisfied. It had all gone to plan. There was a mood of jocularity, camaraderie. We'd got our salmon; now was the time to head home, we were done. I was proud and excited to have been part of the team that had pulled it off. My fears had been unfounded. Father knew what he was doing.

On the way back someone else carried the West of England sack. It had got too heavy for me. I was up ahead of the others. The light being some way behind me, I was in near darkness. The others walked in silence, but the throw of light made big shadows swing from every tree. A hedge, planted atop an earth bank, ran alongside. I was looking for the break that I knew was coming up, where animals had made a gap. I clambered over and down the other side. I could smell the fox that would have gone before me.

Then, out of the darkness, there appeared boots, legs, the knees of men: they came from left and right. I could hear their sudden, low grunts as they saw me. They didn't shout; they didn't want to alert the others. They were shapes in the dark, pale faces and hands showing up before the rest of their bodies materialized. I dropped to the ground, pumped full of adrenalin, just as they came at me. I scooted forwards on hands and knees, between their legs. Sticks swiped at me, coming from all ways. I didn't stop to think of the blows raining down on my back, the hurt didn't matter; I only had to escape. At the same time I let out a shout. I wanted to warn the others that we were in trouble.

All this happened in seconds, although it felt like an age. Then I was on my feet and running as fast as I could, straight into the middle of this dead-level field next to the river. I could run for long distances, fast. It wasn't the first time I'd been caught by the bailiffs and it wouldn't be the last. Once, in years to come, I'd be running from bailiffs with another lad, not so quick as me, and I put him in the brambles, just like a deer hides her calf in undergrowth if she has to run. So, that night, I knew that if I was running no one could catch me. It was the others I was more worried about. Had they been got? I should stop and look back . . .

In the middle of the field was a 'moute' – our word for a tree stump. It's a favourite place for wrens to nest. This one had been washed down here by the floods. The year before, in 1951, the town of Lynmouth had been flooded. The river Lyn, swollen with rain, had burst a natural dam and sent a torrent of water into the town. Many people had been killed. The same rains had washed this moute out of the ground and left it in this valley; now it was my hiding place. I slid in behind it, panting hard, and turned to see what had happened to the others.

The enormous lamp acted like a floodlight on a stage. I could see everything as clear as day. The bailiffs had their torches on now, too, and blades of light criss-crossed the scene. In among this light show people were fighting in hand-to-hand combat. My father fought with Mr Willmotts, the water bailiff. I could see their arms and legs windmilling as they rained blows on one another and struggled to find a grip. As if in slow motion, they both toppled over and into the river.

I ran.

For a mile and a half, in the pitch black, scared to death, I ran for home. When I came down into Brayford the road brought me out in front of the Guardsman's Door, the entrance to the old hut that the Home Guard had used during the war, my father among them. There, luckily, I came across Mr Maddox. Perhaps he'd been alerted by the noise and had come out to see what the fuss was about. In any case, somehow he'd found out what was happening. Now he stopped me, told me not to go over the bridge towards home. If I did, I'd be caught. He sent me up towards Broomhill Villas and advised me to hide there till morning.

So I couldn't go home. Instead I had to throw myself on the mercy of friends and neighbours. At Broomhill Villas lived the White family, who had previously lived next door to us. I ran to the front door and practically beat it down with fright. Mr White opened up, and took in the fact that a lad he knew, a friend of his own children, was standing soaking wet and shaking, in the middle of the night.

'What's happened?' he asked.

'My father and the bailiffs are fighting . . . and I ran and looked back and I saw them falling into the river . . . I can't go home, they're waiting for me . . . so I came here . . .' I couldn't get the words out fast enough.

He was already taking me by the shoulder and pulling me into the house. 'Get up the stairs and go in the door on the right-hand side.' I went, glad to be out of sight and to be safe, but in a state of panic about the others. What had happened to Father? My last sight of him had been that tumbling windmill of arms and legs, brightly lit, as he and the water bailiff fell into the river. Where was he now? Drowned? Hurt? Under arrest?

As it happened, he'd got clean away. They'd searched, and when they didn't find him they'd sent men to stake out our house, back and front, waiting for him and me to return. But he was already inside. He'd got back before them. They were out in the cold, staring in every direction, looking up every path leading to the house, while he was just twitching the curtains to one side, safe in the warm and dry. He'd put one over on them that night. Again.

Meanwhile, in the Whites' house, I climbed the stairs, still muddy and wet and scared. Either the bailiffs had seen the light or someone from the village had informed on us.

At the top of the stairs I turned right as instructed and found myself in the familiar bedroom of the White children. There were three of them, in three beds. They woke and had to be told what had happened.

I moved from one bed to the other to the next and then the first one again. I couldn't sleep. I couldn't help remembering Father cartwheeling with Mr Willmotts through the air. I imagined him pulled from the river, drowned. The next moment I pictured him badly injured, unable to walk, not the same man as the father I knew and loved. I thought he'd been pinned to the ground, the bailiffs twisting his arm behind his back. He'd have been arrested, hauled to the police station, locked away ... When I did fall asleep, I dreamed so vividly that I sleepwalked around the room.

The next morning, at six a.m., Mr White woke me up and said, 'Right, boy, you'd better be off home.' In borrowed clothes I walked to High Bray, back over the bridge where we'd started out from the night before, through the village. Had any of these houses told on us, I wondered? I'd never find out.

Father was arrested, eventually. He was taken to court and fined twenty pounds, which was a lot of money in those days. It would have bought you a dozen salmon. He and I got our names in the papers. I can remember the headline that described my escape: 'BOY DISAPPEARS IN DARKNESS'.

Learning, but not the sort you get in class

"Hanging off the tip of my finger by its fine, very sharp teeth was a river eel.**"**

At the age of fourteen I was only a year away from leaving school, but I was more often than not absent from class. I had the strange idea that I'd rather be working and earning a few shillings than sat in a classroom where I was good for nothing except creating mischief. The Attendance Officer was called Mr Short and he waited at the bus stop to count off those who'd gone to school, so that he could give the headmaster a list of those who hadn't. The headmaster would post a letter to the parents of absconders. Those letters came often to our house, asking after my whereabouts.

There were better, more exciting things to do. We built dams across the river Bray, hauling the biggest stones we could lift out of the pit and threading them along the stickles at the back, and then filling in the gaps with smaller stones and pushing what we called clats – the top layer of earth, held together by grass – into the holes to make it watertight. The water level in the pit rose, and taking out the bigger stones to build the dam also helped make it better for swimming. We spent hours – the Smith boys, my cousin Ronnie Moule, Ian Prosser, Barrie Bailey, the White family, Clifford and Derek Wilmott and me – in and out of the water, the sun on our backs, larking about, skimming stones and swinging on ropes.

On one side of the river was a screen of trees; on our side was a clear bank with that open, level field next to it, which gave us plenty of space. Kingfishers bored holes in the bank to make their nests and they could be seen, a flash of colour, shy and quick, up and down the river. Sand martins were also a common sight; they're like house martins but browner on their backs and they build their nests in a hole in a clay bank instead of under the eaves of houses. More rare were the dippers, flying to and fro; they made their nests under a moute or on a ledge under a bridge, looking similar to oversized wrens' nests.

We waded in the water, turning up stones to find moneygrubs, otherwise known as dumpheads – little fish about two and a half inches long with outsized heads, which we would use to prick onto our night hooks, aiming to catch the biggest trout, the so-called cannibal trout, which were known to eat their own kind. We knew where they lived: in the rush of dark water over at the furthest edge of the pit, where the current was deep and steady and undisturbed, up against the ditch stones which lined the bank at this point, underneath the shade of the trees. I once made my way there, the level of the water rising slowly to my waist and the cold even in summer beginning to grip, just at the same time as the stones underfoot were more slippery and the water heavier around my legs, making it more difficult to balance. It was expected of me to take things out of the river, tickle trout, and so on – it was something the others looked to me for. I didn't want to let them down; I thought I'd find us one of these big cannibal trout right now in broad daylight, instead of waiting for the night lines maybe to bring us one.

Standing and facing upstream in the dark swirl of water, I reached down under the surface and explored the ditch stones, looking for clefts and holes and over-hangs where the trout might be hiding. I leaned over further; the water was pouring past my ears, up to my mouth.

I pushed my hand into a little hole between the stones and felt the side of a trout. I could stroke the smooth, cold side of its belly, but there was no way I could find its gill with my finger to hook it out. I moved my finger from side to side, reaching as far as I could into the gap. It would be facing upstream, so I pressed harder in that direction. The next I knew, I'd pushed my finger into the creature's mouth and it felt like nothing on earth. There was a needle-sharp pain in my finger and I yelled and pulled out my hand and stood up all at the same time. Hanging off the tip of my finger by its fine, very sharp teeth was a river eel.

Of course we knew about eels – we'd clatted for eels before. This involved finding muddy water – it had to be muddy so they couldn't see – and then dangling a bunch of worms wrapped up in a ball of cotton. The eels smelled the worms and struck, but their very fine teeth got caught in the cotton. You could lift out more than one eel at a time that way, and use the same worms again and again. But this wasn't how you should catch an eel, not with its teeth in the end of your finger.

I danced about on the shingles at the back of the pit, shouting and hollering at the top of my voice and shaking my hand like crazy, all at the same time. The others rushed over to see what it was. I shook my whole arm so vigorously that the eel had no choice but to be thrown off and it went flying through the air, still writhing and twisting, and landed on the bank. We were after it, scrambling up there and kneeling down in a circle to watch. It writhed so hard it looked like it was going to tie itself in knots. It struck a deal more fear in us than any fish could do. Some of the others had made bows and arrows and, in the way that boys do, they aimed at the eel and tried to shoot it. Of course this didn't work; the arrows slid off harmlessly. In the end we killed it by hitting it on the back of the head with a stone. This took some doing. I've learned subsequently that the best way of killing an eel is to hit it on the tail. This shocks it right through its body.

We picked up the dead eel. It measured three feet. We headed back to the village with our prize, not sure what on earth we could do with it. I looked at the deep puncture wounds in my finger. Red pricks of blood and bruises showed where the eel had bitten. In the event they'd take a long time to heal and cause me a lot of pain.

The first house we came across, we showed them the eel. Mr Clarke lived at the end of the same row as Uncle Harry and the Wilmotts. He was quite an old man, short and stubby. He took one look at the eel and offered us two shillings for it, and ate it for his supper.

Poaching was a way of life, but it was a land of plenty, as the Bible says, both in the rivers and on the land. Today it's different. Fish are more scarce. There isn't the same sense of bounty, which we thoughtlessly took advantage of, especially in those years during the war and just afterwards when there was rationing, and genuine hunger in every household. There are some things we did that, with hindsight, I shouldn't have done. It's a question of sportsmanship; even among poachers there's the question of what is fair game. For the last twenty-five years or more

I haven't poached, and I've saved the lives of any number of creatures. And I hope the films I make arouse in the audience a sense of wonder that will encourage all of us to appreciate the wildlife that shares our countryside. It has become a question of conservation, of both the creatures themselves and their habitat. Any study of nature will show you countless examples of how, once a particular species becomes more dominant than it should be, other species suffer. They fail to compete, and become extinct. The species that's become too dominant, too successful, is ourselves. Throughout the world we threaten and destroy other species on a grand scale. It will take all our resolve, our good will, energy and commitment, to control the careless plunder of our own habitat.

If there was only one good reason to bunk off school, that was the nit-nurse, Miss Edwards. She was a fearsome figure, very strict, and masculine in appearance. She wore a man's suit – trousers, waistcoat, a jacket and tie, the works. Her hair was cut short. 'One of those sort, I expect,' said my sister. I didn't know what she meant. 'Stand up straight! Look ahead! Chin up!' She stood you upright and pulled your hair all different ways, hunting for nits, shining a torch at your scalp. It was agony to have her grab the hair behind your ears and yank it up so she could stare in closely, looking for the stubborn tiny eggs or the crawling bugs. I can still hear the sound of her breathing. I don't think the nits dared come to our school, either.

Another reason to avoid school was that any day I did go seemed to end in more trouble. If I didn't go, there were less beatings and arguments and tickings off, all round.

But the third and best reason for not going to school was because I started to work more regularly for Jim Venn.

In fact, I knew Jim's mother before I knew him. Old Granny Slater was her name. She took it on herself to keep an eye on the church and graveyard. She lived close alongside and regarded it as her special duty to stop any irreverent behaviour. Right beside the cemetery – where I helped my dad dig graves – was a mound covered in laurel bushes. It was where the village's plague victims had been buried, apparently, back in the 1600s, but it was where we now liked to build hides. This involved a certain amount of playing in the graveyard itself, and on the scaffolding which was put up against the church as it underwent repairs. Old Granny Slater would see us playing on hallowed ground, taking the Lord's name in vain, so to speak, and she would stride up to the church-yard, carrying a shotgun and dressed as a German soldier.

She'd plant both feet square, aim into the sky and fire both barrels, to frighten us off. We'd jump from the scaffold or duck out from behind the graves and run for the safety of our dens in the laurel bushes.

Her son Jim was a carpenter and smallholder, who would have been around sixty back then. He had a carpentry shop in an old shed down near Mill Farm, where he made coffins – and they were done in solid oak and elm in those days. He had a forge fire in there, to heat up the pitch he used to seal the coffins. Nowadays a dead body is treated with an injection which prevents leakage of body fluids but no such thing existed at that time and so coffins had to be sealed. He'd heat the pitch until it was liquid, then paint it on to the inside of the wood.

I began to help Jim Venn both on his smallholding and with the coffins, sorting and cutting timber, and so on. He was a laugh, was Jim, and I grew to like him more and more. Of course, there was plenty of gallows humour in making coffins.

Jim said to me, 'Hop in this one, Johnny, try it out for size.' The coffin lay on trestles, smelling of freshly turned wood. I climbed in.

'Lie down, then,' said Jim.

I did so, and crossed my arms over my chest. It was a bit odd to be lying in someone's coffin. You certainly felt your own death might be just round the corner.

'I'm not sure I've made it deep enough,' he said. 'Hold still . . . while I just see if the lid fits on.' Before I knew it he'd picked up the lid and slid it over me. What was more, a dozen bangs of the hammer told me he'd clatted the nails in; the thing was shut fast. I was in a coffin, lid nailed down and all. I couldn't see a thing. It was pitch black. The wood was an inch from my nose and the sides pressed at my elbows. I felt real terror. I hollered and shouted as loud as my lungs would let me. He was laughing. I was only in there for about ten seconds, I'd guess, but I've never been so frightened before or since. If he'd lifted the lid off and found me dead of fright, after all, it would hardly have been surprising.

Jim Venn bought the Old Rectory, after Revd Grainger died. This property, as I said, was just below ours, further down the slope. It included a clutch of stone-built barns with slate roofs set around a cobble yard, and a number of acres of land. He had a collie dog that moved from one spot to another around the yard herding the chickens, when it wasn't needed to move the few sheep and cows Jim kept. I helped with milking – washing the teats and then milking by hand into buckets, the old-fashioned way. It's incredible to think of the work that was done by hand back then. Sheep-shearing was done with hand shears. Any wounds to the animal were sealed with oil. A machine arrived for shearing one day, but it didn't have an electric motor, it was mechanical, and it was my job to turn the handle that made the blades scissor back and forth. It seemed to us a very advanced technology, at the time.

Jim also had an enormous beast of a carthorse, or so it seemed to us, called Violet, who was used like a tractor to work the land. Violet was in fact a perfectly ordinary pony, but to us she looked as tall as a house, and as broad. She could work all day without breaking sweat. She moved with a stately, clumping gait, and it took her a full 10 yards to turn round and face the opposite direction, a bit like an oil tanker.

Jim had Violet in the field once, with just a loose rope around her neck, no bridle or saddle. There was a gang of us there, and he suggested we should go for a ride, not one by one but all up there together, like Uncle Tom Cobbley and all. He put up Pat and Joe Moule, my cousins, on her back, and then me as well, and then Mary Tucker, and then my sisters Julie and Susan, and right at the front went little Ruth Maddox. It was like a whole row at school assembly. Violet patiently carried us along. It was slippery without a saddle. We tracked along the side of a long cleave, as we call it – a steep valley. Jim Venn walked alongside Violet's flanks, holding on to the loose bit of rope around her neck.

Then he suffered one of his fits of good humour – he took it on himself to let go of the rope and whack Violet's rump, hard. It had a dramatic effect. Violet leapt forward and plunged down the steep slope at a full gallop. We were immediately at sixes and sevens, clinging on to each other and trying to stay on. It was like being on a fairground slide when you drop vertically, it took our breath away. Joe Moule dived off to save himself. I lost balance and tumbled to the ground and pulled Pat Moule with me. My sister Julie fell off. So did Susan and Mary Tucker. Within a few seconds we were all sitting on our arses and watching Violet canter faster and faster down the slope. The smallest of all of us was still clinging on – Ruth Maddox. She was at the front and had the mane to hold on to. Our hearts were in our mouths as we watched this tiny figure bouncing up and down on Violet's back. She went all the way down to the bottom. When the horse reached the more level ground she veered off left, slowing to a trot. Ruth slid off. She was safe.

Jim Venn was still laughing.

There were plenty of things we did as a gang, up to no good. Old Mr Huxtable ran the village shop; quite a small man, he sort of waddled along, always a bit slow, in his farmer's cap. We'd go into his old, dark place, five or six of us, down the gloomy corridor to where he lingered among his dusty tins, and so on, and we'd ask for a packet of crisps. He'd lean down under the counter to fetch it, out of sight for a full half-minute – once you took into account he had to clutch his back, grunt and groan a few times, find the crisps, and pull himself upright again. So we could safely take an extra bottle of cherryade from the shelf and steal it away.

However, when we grew older we had different needs. We fancied a bottle of cider each. We knew where the alcohol was kept, in an old granary store around the back of the shop. We'd have to wait until he was off the premises.

Mr Huxtable was a chapel man. On those particular nights, religiously at six p.m., he and his wife dressed in their best clothes and walked to chapel. They were certain to be away for at least an hour and a half. We watched them go and then we made our move. There was a high gate we had to get past. I was bumped up, and soon got over that. Wooden steps led down to the granary building. I crept down. It was pitch black and drizzling rain. When I was in the old granary store it was even darker; I had to feel my way among the gas canisters and the odds and sods he kept in there. But I knew where the cider was. Eventually I felt my way to the right spot. I took down seven bottles, one for each of us. Moments later I was out of the granary and on to the rickety wooden stairs again. I came to the high gate, but there was no way I could climb over carrying seven bottles of cider. I found a gap and eager hands took the bottles from me as I slid them through. Then I could climb over.

We had seven whole bottles – one each, as we'd

planned. It was a scandal. Half running and half walking we headed out of the village, hiding the bottles in our clothes. We crossed the bridge and turned left, out on the road towards Liddicott. Up there was Jim Venn's carpentry shop, where I helped him make coffins. Outside the shop was a lean-to which he used to store wood and suchlike. It was a place we often went to get out of the rain if we were courting, or to smoke cigarettes. It was the place to go. We sat down on a plank of wood and took out our dark brown bottles, ready to become proper drinkers like our fathers and grandfathers before us. Father, in fact, had given up alcohol by now. He'd drunk quite heavily when he was younger and it meant he lost his temper, so he'd ditched the stuff.

One by one, my friends drank from the bottles we'd stolen. It felt like we were becoming men. I lifted my bottle and took a swig – and spat it out, straight off. They had cider; I'd somehow got a bottle of useless sodding vinegar.

In 1954, aged fifteen, I left school and went to work for Mr Tucker. He lived in the same village and had a big farm by Exmoor standards – two hundred acres plus other bits and pieces of rented ground and some grazing up on the moor. There were several others working with me. Ruth Maddox – she who'd managed to stay on the galloping horse – worked in the dairy. We'd milk the cows, carry the buckets down and empty them into a big stainless-steel container which fed the milk through the cooler. From the cooler it went straight into bottles, and the bottles were taken by Ruth and Mr Tucker and loaded into a little white Ford van, which was then driven round the village, making deliveries. There wasn't any pasteurizing. It was straight from the cow to the doorstep.

I was mostly out on the land. Ern Johns also worked for Mr Tucker and a lot of the time I was alongside him. There was an old Fordson Major tractor, the type with the wide wings, and I learned how to plough with that. Hoeing mangolds and swedes was done by hand or we used the carthorse with drags and chain harrows. In winter there was hedging to be done – casting up the banks and filling in the gaps. It was my job to be down at the bottom with a big twelve-prong stone fork, pitching up stones or cutting out clats and throwing them up to make the bank. Nowadays it's all done with diggers, which scoop up the earth with the bucket and push it into place, but back then the banks were all hand-built, using the clats of earth like bricks. It was hard work. When the bank was up to the correct height, the last clat would be set upside down. The density of the grass roots in the clat made it near enough waterproof. Then an inch of earth would be laid on top of that. Meanwhile the hedges on the tops of the banks would have to be laid. That was long hours of work also. The thickest stems were cut down to length while the more slender ones were cut halfway through so they could be bent over and laid flat, held in place with crooks – the pegs which we made on the spot with our hooks, using the clefts of branches. When a beech stem is cut only half way through it will keep growing beyond the cut, so the hedge grows thicker year by year. The excess growth was trimmed with a hook. It looked beautiful, did a well-laid hedge. Nowadays it's all done by machine and it's very quick, but it doesn't look as good. It used to take us three weeks to do a hedge, whereas a whole farm can be done now in a week.

After working alongside Ern Johns for around a year, a lot of it making good the hedges and banks, and always with myself toiling away down below with Ern doing the smart work up on top, I was getting restless. One day we were up behind the Poltimore Arms, at Yard Down. It was raining and I was fed up. The old twelve-prong stone fork was slippery in my hands and the clats of earth were heavy with water, as it began to rain harder. I wanted to be doing more useful, skilled work. I asked Ern a couple of times if I could be promoted, do what he was doing. He turned me down. I began to push it a bit. 'How come you never let me bloody go up there, Ern? I'm never going to learn anything stuck down here.'

'You'll learn by watching me do it, boy.'

'I bluddy won't, I'll only ever learn aught if I get up and do it.'

'The day will come when you will. But it'll be me that tells you when.'

'Today is the day, Ern. It is, true.'

I carried on in this vein – how it riled me that I was his slave, doing all the lifting. Was he afraid of a bit of hard work, then? Could he not handle the strain?

I made one gripe too many. There was a moment's silence. Then Ern Johns leaped off the bank and suddenly we were fighting. I was very fit and strong, but in no time he had me on my backside. He pinned me down in the ditch that ran alongside the bank. It was raining hard and it was close to being a stream. I could feel the cold water enter at my collar and run all down through my clothes and out the bottom of my trousers. Ern Johns sat on me with his forearm across my neck, and from close range he swore right at me, 'You do what you'm bluddy told. I am the man in charge here and I will have you know that, and not ever forget it. I will tell you *when* you work, *where* you work, and *what* bluddy work you do. D'you hear?'

I never argued with Ern Johns again. He was a tough, strong man as was proven to me many times. When I came across Mr Tucker's old carthorse dead in the gateway, I half expected Ern to be able to pick it up and carry it down to the kennels himself, but we had to use the low-loader. He was quick and fearless as well as strong. At that time farmers could control their own deer and laid snares in the racks – the gaps in the hedge where the deer passed through. These snares were made of substantial gauge wire, around ⅛ inch thick. The deer would run through and be caught by the neck, like in a lasso. Ern asked me to check the wires. I went out to see a hind standing a full 15 feet from the hedge. It couldn't have been caught in the wire, I thought, if it was way out there – but then why was it just waiting in the open? As I approached it ran, and the wire sprang out of the grass and whipped tight, and of course the deer was forced to run in a circle. Before I knew it the wire swept round and knocked me flat. I was lucky not to be badly hurt. A wire moving like that, with that amount of power behind it, works like a cheese-cutter; it could have taken my legs off. I ran back to tell Ern Johns that we had a big problem, that there was a full-size hind running wild on the end of this length of wire. We'd have to shoot it, no one would get near.

'That . . . is no problem at all,' he said. And without a moment's thought he strode out to that field and walked straight down the wire. He was quick enough to dance round it, not allowing it to catch him. He walked up to the deer, wrestled it to the ground and cut its throat without hesitation. 'There you are,' he said. 'Not a problem.' We brought it back to the farm and took out its stomach. He gave me some liver.

It will sound shocking to some but we lived in that sort of way. It was what was done. It was how we came by our meat, it was part of our livelihoods. For Ern Johns it was a normal thing to kill an animal. He was one of those employed by folk to kill their pigs. It was our way of life and not a scrap was wasted. It is the way of some animals to kill and eat other animals; we were no different.

In later years, Ern lived on his own, not able to see too well. He couldn't even watch television. By then I was taking my wildlife videos to Barnstaple market, which was near where he lived, and I can remember how he'd come along in his cap and dark-rimmed glasses, pushing his walking frame – and he'd always buy copies of my films. He'd play the video just to listen to them; he said he liked the sound of my voice because it kept him company and it reminded him of when he was young. I always talked too much when we worked together, he said.

He died only last year, 2005, aged ninety-four. I was on the way to his funeral when there was an accident on the North Devon link road that prevented quite a few of us from reaching the service on time. I bitterly resented that. I wanted to say goodbye to a man I'd liked a great deal, whom I'd worked alongside for two years, and who had frightened the shits out of me. Rest in peace, Ern Johns.

By now I'd grown pretty strong myself, but it was Uncle Arthur, in fact, who started the whole boxing thing. He'd learned to fight in the army and had the gloves, and so on. And then when I was about sixteen my dad started to teach me to box, in my turn. At around eleven every night my dad and I would put on gloves and face up to each other. Right there in the kitchen he taught me to keep guard, to block shots, to duck and weave, how to jab and how to put together combinations of punches. For ages, try as I might, I never went through his guard. Any punch I threw was pushed aside by his gloves or skidded off his forearms. If I aimed for his chin then my glove hit thin air and like as not, a second later, I'd feel the smack of his glove against the side of my head or against my body as his counter-punch scored a direct hit.

There was this one time, when Mother was in bed and my sisters too, except maybe for the older ones who were out courting. Father and I danced around the kitchen. We knocked against furniture, stumbled backwards, lurched forwards. There were smiles and laughter, then it turned serious for a while, then went back to being light-hearted. Time went on – it was past midnight. I became more determined to make something count. This was the Cat, the Powder Monkey – the man who'd taught me everything I knew. It would be a serious triumph if I could put one shot on target. Father drew breath to say something and at the same time I powered through with my right hand and tagged him square on the jaw, a bit too hard. The second my glove connected I felt a plumb dread and fear in my stomach. I'd hit him. That wasn't good news; I wasn't going to get away with that. A shocked look flashed across his face. It wasn't part of the plan that I should grow big enough and quick enough to lay one on him. I was seventeen; he was in his forties. He cursed. I stepped back, put up my guard. His anger quickened – he was coming for me. I went to take another step backwards but couldn't. The kitchen cupboard was against my back.

I didn't see his fist start out, but I knew it was coming because of the sudden clench in his expression, so I ducked sideways. Sure enough his glove whistled past my ear. I felt the wind of it and heard the grunt as he gave it all his strength. He'd aimed to hurt me; he wanted to teach me a lesson. The next moment there was an almighty crash and the sound of breaking crockery. The cupboard behind me was built into the wall of the kitchen, and my lurch sideways meant that Father's glove missed me and instead burst clean through the cupboard door and smashed the dishes stacked inside.

Upstairs, Mother heard the shout and the sound of broken plates and cups. She hurried downstairs to see what had happened. Her face was pale; she was worried someone was hurt. 'What's going on?' she called. But she could see at a glance what was wrong. Father still hadn't managed to pull his fist out of the cupboard. It was stuck fast, wedged in there among the dishes. He was cursing, 'I'll learn you . . . !'

That was unfair. He'd taught me to box and, guess what, I was learning. He couldn't complain. When he'd calmed down we unlaced his glove so he could pull out his hand, and the glove dropped out the other side of the cupboard door. We cleaned out the broken crockery and pushed the panel up together again so it more or less did the job it was meant to do, but with a couple of big splits down the middle.

My father was a stern man, quick to discipline us. That belt, the one with the big buckle, would come off darn quick when there was some incident or other he disapproved of. And then I or my sisters would feel the sting of it, sometimes even the buckle end. More often you'd feel the clip of his hand on the back of your head. It stunned you, momentarily. I've been knocked down by my father. I've cowered away from him, afraid. He once upended a plate of stew on my head when I'd complained about it always being rabbit stew on Thursdays and I didn't like it any more. By today's standards that kind of punishment would be frowned on. It would be thought cruel. But more often than not I needed some truth knocking into me, and it worked. He gave me so much; I followed in his footsteps in both my work and my interests. I loved him without question. The punishments were for a reason and taught me where the boundaries lay, when the cheek was too much, when I'd stepped over the mark, which was often enough. The leatherings and the clips around the ear taught me that just as surely as he taught me how to tickle trout or aim a rifle, or box. He was a good father; I was lucky. He had a quick temper but he gave his children – six of us – everything he had it in his power to give. Children like boundaries to run up against when they are growing and they like to feel that they are listened to, that they are important enough to be taught. Against every brief second that he might have raised a hand to us must be set the many hours that he gave to us. He put food in the larder, he taught us all we needed to know to get on in life. I loved both my parents and wouldn't change one thing about my childhood. I count myself a lucky man.

That split panel in the door of the kitchen cupboard stayed like that for some while. I would meet and court my wife Julie and the cupboard stayed broke. When I was nineteen I'd go to Hong Kong on National Service and when I came back two years later it was still broke.

Top left: *My mother Joyce, with her beloved cat Stumpy. She always wore that apron or one just like it around the house – she liked to keep everything to hand in its huge pockets.*

Top right: *My father Walter, with his cups from Brayford flower and vegetable show – it was a struggle to break through the usual ring of winners but he managed it.*

Bottom: *With my sisters Susan (left) and Julie, the ones nearest to my age – I turned to my sisters for help when I fell out with Father in my teenage years.*

Left: *Raymond White (standing) pushing me round at Guy Fawkes time. We were always up to some sort of mischief but it was Raymond's brother David who got stuck up the chimney when we went searching for eggs.*

Right: *In my churchgoing days – I even sang in the choir.*

Below left: *Violet, Jim Venn's horse we all rode on – we were sure she was as big as a carthorse.*

Below right: *Boys from the village – we were the bees' knees with our quiffed hair and our wide collars, chasing all the girls in town.*

Main photograph: *Brayford, in the valley just below where I was born, and where I spent much of my time.*

Inset: *Raymond Penfold, Uncle Harry, Fred Welsh and myself beside the navvy, a machine for loading stones onto the lorry. Fred Welsh was the driver of this machine.*

Main photograph: *Rock drilling – I'd graduated from using a harness to just a rope as I dug the rocks from the quarry face – a dangerous business. The drop is 270 feet, beneath us. The other man is Tony Linders, quarry foreman and best man at my wedding.*

Main photograph: *The parade ground in Hong Kong –*
the heat was unbearable when we did drill in the afternoons.

Below left: SS Oxfordshire, *the boat that took us to Hong Kong.*

Below centre: *Inspection day, standing next to 'five-five' guns at the*
Hong Kong base.

Below right: *Unscrewing the tops of the 100lb shells – it was heavy*
work to move them around.

Left: *Julie, my future wife (centre) aged thirteen at South Molton carnival around the time we first met – I didn't really notice her until later.*

Left and above: *Julie and me – I courted her more determinedly than ever when I got back from the army.*

Above left: *She must have said yes – but it took some persuading to get Julie to agree, never mind her dad.*

Above right: *Picnicking on the moor with our sons Craig and Stuart, I felt on top of the world.*

Top: *Relaxing together in the sunshine.*

Main photograph: *Crossing Tarr Steps.*

Inset: *Showing a film crew how I used to poach salmon – I put this one back, of course.*

Main photograph: *Sawing the end of a fir tree – I loved being my own boss. Every hour I worked was more money in my pocket to take home to Julie and the boys.*

Inset: *Putting Stuart to work early. This was a Monterey pine tree, huge.*

Left: *With Craig (left) and Stuart at the Christmas after my accident. I was barely able to hold myself together in front of the boys.*

Below: *The Chariot – after the success of showing my film in Bishops Nympton, I went further afield across the south west, selling them at local fairs and shows.*

Right: *With the lambs from Sindercombe. I was grateful to Herbert Thorne for the job at Sindercombe as I recovered from my accident. Just being around the animals seemed to help my recovery.*

Left: *With the Reverend Pennington and his daughter. The Rev. changed my life completely, helping me out of depression (and even stopping me smoking!).*

Below: *With my first video camera – I really got the bug after using Roger Gregory's camera, even though it wasn't a great success in producing a film.*

I'd put the fear of God into local landowners and bailiffs with my poaching and carrying-on all through my twenties, and no one mended that panel; every time I visited Mother and Father there it was, just the same. I'd marry Julie and have two sons, and still that kitchen cupboard door stayed exactly as it was the night my father put his fist through it. My mother grew old and Father died, the youthful strength and power and anger that had burst the cupboard door just a memory, withered away by the passing years. Still that split panel waited to be mended.

I visited the house recently with a film crew. We'd had to obtain permission from the new owners, who'd lived there since Mother's death three years previously. When I walked in, it was as if the whole of my childhood rushed back. The happiness and the trouble. Strife and hunger; excitement and plenty. The riches of experience. Here were the stairs that we'd clattered up and down, day and night. The floor across which had crawled all the black beetles, Mother putting down cucumber skin to poison them. It no longer had a lino covering, it was tiled. Right there had stood the farmhouse table around which we'd eaten that rabbit stew on Thursdays. Now in its place stood a circular pine table.

And there was the cupboard built into the wall, just as before, but the broken panel had been replaced. The entire cupboard had been painted over. This last sign of my father had gone. He'd grown old and died, and the cupboard was mended.

I'd be happy, God knows, if someone told me I'd been as good a father to my sons as he was to me.

Starting work for real

“ *Boom!* A shower of rocks blew out of the face of the quarry. **”**

In 1956, aged seventeen, I began work at Nott's Quarries. Father had spoken to Stewart Nott and got me the start.

So he and I walked to work together, the same way he'd done for many years already, like I described before: out the house, turn right in the lane, up to the church and through the gate. Then we'd track across the bottom corner of the graveyard, over the step in the bank and down that quite steep drop of land, looking over the valley cut out by the river Bray, heading downstream. Over the river – using the bridge he'd made himself – to the quarry, a big Exmoor hill that had been blasted near enough in half by the explosions, a sheer cliff of bluestone chased back, dark grey in colour, excavated out of the surrounding woodland, with the machinery at the bottom which would crush the rocks into different grades of chip, gravel or stone, and the lorries hauling it away.

I was scared of heights but found myself working on

ledges 300 feet up the side of the cliff. For three months I was terrified. We'd drill holes four feet apart, using hammer drills driven by compressed air, similar to the ones you see digging up roads. Victor powder or gelignite would be used as charges. Pills, we called them, around three inches in circumference. Drill the hole, drop in the pills. In the last pill we'd fix the detonator. On top of that went stone dust or clay pills, tamped down firmly to keep it airtight. The wires sticking up from each charge were joined together in a circle, and then we'd run the pair of wires up to the top, to the plunger, which was sited in a little shed or behind a tree, depending. When someone's hand was on the T-shaped handle of the plunger, the fire-horn would be sounded as a warning. Two men on traffic duty in the lane below would halt any cars coming through. The handle went down – *boom!* A shower of rocks blew out of the face of the quarry. The bigger ones we split open where they lay with what we called plasters – gelignite pads with a detonator stuck in them. The fuse gave us two and a half minutes to get out of danger. Then we went in with bars and levered down the rock that had split. Blasting took place maybe twice a day. It was heavy work and it scared me. You don't forget that kind of thing – it keeps you awake all night you're so frightened. When you're 100 feet up a precipice, ripping out stones with a bar, attached to a rope and harness, it's not a good idea to be bad at heights.

And there were stories that told you it wasn't the safest work. In the stores worked a man nicknamed Foxy, I'm not sure why. He had one arm, which of course wasn't a problem, working in the stores. You went to Foxy if you needed a bag of tea, or some paraffin, or some oil, and he could lift it on to the counter all right with his one hand. But he'd previously worked in the quarry itself. He'd been on the plasters – those smaller pads of gelignite, as I've described, which you stuck on to the rocks to split them open. The trick was to lay quite a few at the same time, but it was important to remember that you only had two and a half minutes to get out of the way before they blew. The other critical instruction as far as plasters were concerned was not to return too quickly. There was a chance one or other of them wouldn't have gone off and you had to make sure, like with fireworks, that there was a safe interval before anyone returned.

Foxy had the one empty sleeve tucked in his pocket because he went back too early. One of the plasters blew right beside him. It took his left arm clean off and threw it some distance through the air, out of sight. A team of men – Father included – immediately picked up Foxy from where he'd fallen and carried him 200 yards out across the road and along the way a bit to the tin shed occupied by the blacksmith. In there he was laid on the bench, and the forge fire was stoked up. Quick as possible a steel rod was made red hot, then it was laid against all the cords and arteries that dangled from the blasted stump at his shoulder, fizzling them all up, cauterizing them.

It was Father who was set the task of going back to find Foxy's arm – because it would have to be buried and Father was the gravedigger, after all. He scouted around some distance from the site of the explosion and eventually found it. As he told it, the most remarkable thing to him was how heavy it weighed. He took it out to the waste tip where the stone dust was pushed into a great heap, and he buried it there. He thought that would be the end of it, but two weeks later he was required by some regulation or other to dig it up again. It was no longer such a fresh item as when he'd last seen it, as might be imagined. He dropped it in a West of England sack, just like a big salmon, and carried it up to High Bray churchyard and buried it in a plot of its own, in sacred ground, where it might wait for its owner to catch up with it.

Years passed. Foxy did fine with his one arm, working in the stores. However, when he died, for some reason he wasn't reunited with the arm in High Bray churchyard. He was buried about a mile away across the valley, as a bird would fly, at a place called Charles. So he never was put back together again.

It had been that one careless action – returning to his plasters too early – that had put Foxy through that traumatic accident. It was dangerous and unforgiving work and anyone would be right to be properly scared of it. Yet after a while you get used to anything. I learned to live with the terror of working high up on a rock face. It wasn't long before I began to do without the harness. Like some of the other men, Father included – the Cat himself – I began to work using only a rope. It gave you a lot more freedom of movement. The only piece of equipment I never did without was that white hard hat. I hadn't caught up with the agility and expertise of Father, and never did, in fact, but I'd learned to swallow my fear and do the work required.

A young lad came to the quarry who was as scared as I was when I'd first arrived. His name was Steve Williams and he became a mate of mine. I still speak to his mum today – a lovely person. As it happened, I was the one detailed to teach him to climb. We were set to work at Gardie's Pit, a smaller quarry away from the main one.

He was the beginner, but I was the one to fall. I was ripping stones out and I went down with a bunch of them, falling 50 feet down a 75 degree slope. One of the boulders that fell with me landed on the inside of my ankle and cut the artery. Uncle Arthur, Fred Welsh and Michael Edwards were the first to reach where I lay, bruised and knocked about with a dramatic amount of blood pouring on to the stones. Father came to the rescue also. They found a big piece of rag and twisted it into a tourniquet and bound it tight around my calf to stop the bleeding.

It wasn't long until I mended. But some years later Steve Williams fell down the exact same slope at Gardie's Pit, and he fell for the same reason: he'd graduated from the harness and worked just with a rope to hand. He had his shirt off – no protection at all. Just as I had been, he was ripping stones out with the bar, and sending them down. He was a fit, good-looking young man, but by the time he reached the bottom he was badly broken. I know that job so well, its dangers, that I can take that fall with him. I can feel every knock, how the cliff tips you end over end, without any control.

Steve Williams died at the bottom of that quarry, in among the stones that had broken him on the way down. He's buried in High Bray churchyard.

Of course there was another potential use for explosives, for those of us who were poachers. Up from the main pit was another, smaller quarry, called Bonnie's Pit, where we were often sent. We were up there one day – Tony Linders, who was the quarry foreman, and myself – and we slipped away to the river with some ammunition. We headed for this spot where a big moute leaned out over the river. We knew there were some big trout that lurked among its roots. I wired the ammo to a stone so it would sink underwater and trimmed the fuse very short. Then we settled down to wait. We didn't want our explosion to be noticed, and so the idea was that we should set it off in among the other blasts, coming from a short way off, at Bonnie's Pit. We listened, we waited. As expected, a series of plasters started blowing. We lit the fuse and tossed our ammo into the water. You'd think the water would put out the fuse, but there's nothing that will stop it burning once it's going. The charge detonated under the water and there was a big *thump* and a huge spray of earth and moute and water went up in the air. I imagine it was like being in the war when a mortar lands nearby.

However, we'd misjudged the amount of ammunition we'd need. The whole bank caved in. There wasn't time to worry about that – the shock wave had travelled through the pit and stunned all the trout. The water was black and muddy. We raced back and waded into the stickles and watched as the fish rose to the surface, showing the whites of their bellies. We were back and forth, water up to our knees, plucking them out as they floated past. We picked up twelve good-sized ones, but suddenly there was this enormous salmon there as well – you wouldn't have expected a salmon in the summertime. It was half stunned, lazy with shock. I immediately forgot about the trout and went to grapple with this 10-pound cock fish. I managed to haul it out. Ten pounds of salmon is quite a thing to handle, slippery as hell.

We put our haul in the usual old West of England sack and made our way back to the main pit. We hid the fish in an old wooden cupboard there, in the room where we made up the plasters, and so on. The cupboard had sliding doors and was used for old nuts and bolts and grease-guns. No one but us looked in there from one week to the next.

Not many minutes later, before we had had a chance to escape with our haul at the end of the working day, we were in this same room when the water bailiff came in. He'd probably seen the bank all blown to hell. For all we knew he might have seen it happen, he was so quick to come up. If he hadn't, then someone had told on us. He began looking around. He saw who was there: Father and I were known poachers. Punch Jury. Terry Taylor. Barry Rippen. Our faces were all blank, of course. The cupboard waited there. The water bailiff sniffed around the room, looked us over. We tried to be as relaxed as possible, but I was sure our lot was up. There was no way his attention wouldn't be drawn to that cupboard.

He began to question us, taking a sarcastic approach. He knew the fish were hidden somewhere. 'Bud,' he said. That was the name most people used for my father. 'What's the difference between a sea trout and a salmon, d'you have an idea?'

'No idea.' My father grinned.

'OK. Johnny, then, d'you know . . . What fish is it that has a square tail?'

'Square tail, Mr Rogers?'

'Yes.'

'I never heard of a fish with no square tail.'

'You don't know much about fish, then? None of you? Bud?' The cupboard was right behind him.

'They swim in the river, I know that much.'

'You wouldn't have heard about an explosion down there at the river, hmmm?'

'We've heard plenty of explosions, we're up here working . . . all day. You sure it wasn't an explosion up here you're talking about?'

'I know what I'm talking about. I know where it was and why it happened and who was responsible.'

The water bailiff had been looking to see if the fish were in our bags, or maybe he thought we'd have them out on the table to gut them. You could see his frustration, but maybe he was a touch nervous too. After all, he was facing up to a bunch of men who were pretty handy with ammunition, hammers and iron bars. He asked his questions, but for whatever reason he didn't go and look in that cupboard. I suppose it didn't look like a larder. He must have thought we'd have kept the fish in among our coats, ready to go home. He left empty-handed. We'd got away with it, again.

By the time I was eighteen I had an explosives licence – this was before I had a driving licence, even. It meant I was entitled to take on explosives work outside the quarry. Ern Parker was my assistant and used to drive me, seeing as he had a driving licence. We'd work on the roads, blowing boulders that were in the way and too big to move with the hydraulic rigs. The Forestry Commission gave us the job of clearing tracks for their vehicles. Farmers wanted tree stumps blown out of the ground. I'd take Father along as well, at times.

One day Ern Parker drove us and our ammunition just a bit out beyond Yard Down, to land belonging to my old employer, Mr Tucker. He wanted a whole row of tree stumps blown out of the ground – around twenty or so, as I remember. Also among our party was another Ern, Ern Dennis, who wanted to come and see how it was done.

I took the bar and approached the first tree stump. 'See,' I said, 'you drive a hole in under the roots at 75 degrees or so. Three of them, in a semi-circle, like that. Which means the stump is blown in that direction . . .' He watched as Ern Parker and myself drove these holes under the moutes and packed them with explosives. Twenty in all. It took a while. 'Now,' I said to Ern Dennis, 'I'm going to trot along all these fuses and we have only two and a half minutes from lighting the first of them to run out the way, OK?'

He nodded.

'I mean really run, mind. Not just a trot. We've got to get our arses well away. Out of here.'

'All right.'

'You want to move off before I start, give yourself time?'

'No, go on. I'll keep up with you.'

I went down to the first in the row of fuses and set it fizzing, moving swiftly from one to the next. Within a minute I'd lit all twenty and was running hard, seeing as how life depended on it. I ran right past Ern Dennis like he was standing still. He certainly wasn't moving fast enough. It didn't seem like he'd quite grasped the urgency of the situation. When I looked back over my shoulder I could see him stumbling along, tree stumps whizzing in all directions. He dropped to all fours – whether he slipped or whether he thought it was better to be low to the ground, I don't know, but it meant he was crawling forwards on hands and knees. On my life, I saw it with my own eyes like something in a comedy film: a chunk of tree whizzed up behind him and hit him square on his backside. It pitched him smartly forwards, nose first, in the mud. He had the good sense to stay lying down and to cover his head with his hands.

When all twenty moutes were blown, there was a sudden, deafening silence. Ern Dennis looked up.

He'd hurt his pride, that was all. We were so

relieved. The tension and anxiety being let go, as it were, gave us a fit of uncontrollable laughter. All three of us, we couldn't stop. We stood looking at Ern's dishevelled, mud-spattered figure clutching his back-side, at the moute lying there, at the other tree trunks dotted about all over the place, and it was the funniest thing ever. We were crying.

There were other outside jobs. We were contracted to blow bedrock out for the South Molton swimming pool. Alongside me on this job was a man whose name I don't remember; I only recall he was a Welshman. We were using cordite – explosive in the form of a long rope, kept wound on a reel. I was preparing and laying the charges and setting them off. It was the Welshman's job to store the ammunition and make sure it was safe. When I got a call from the police asking me to come in immediately, I was filled with dread. What had happened?

I found out: the cordite had not been secured properly the evening before, and a group of schoolgirls had somehow got hold of a reel of it. They unwound it and used it as a skipping rope, a girl at each end and a half-dozen more jumping over the middle. Luckily nothing had happened to set it off. It made my blood run cold. But for the grace of God all those kids would have been maimed or killed. Both myself and the Welshman were fired on the spot, quite rightly, but I kept my licence because on this occasion it hadn't been my responsibility to lock away the ammunition at night.

That was an accident that didn't happen; I wouldn't always be so lucky.

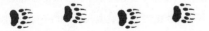

I was older now, and wilder – and I found others who were the same way. The Boyles family lived in a big old cottage at Molland Cross. To look at their place you might guess there was plenty going on. Some of the windows were all filled in with cardboard, slates had flown off the roof and lay in the road, and so on – it had the air of a place held together with string, it was used so much. Vehicles littered the place. Old father Boyles would come back on his motorbike. It was some sort of kit you could buy. If you were unkind you might describe it as a kind of shed fixed to the chassis of the bike, and he used this to carry his six sons and eight daughters with him. It was a notorious vehicle in the neighbourhood, this motorized shed, but you didn't argue with old Mr Boyles. He was a tree man, and the whole family – father and sons – were the handiest men with axes you'd ever meet. My Uncle Tony was once driving a blue Panther motorbike, very smart, no shed attached to it whatsoever, when he was in a collision with Mr Boyles' vehicle, head on. It was a fair old smack and

Uncle Tony's front, the whole of his chest and stomach it looked like, had opened up – blood and gore and so on. It was a grisly sight. Yet Uncle Tony got to his feet and started walking around as if nothing had happened. It turned out he'd been carrying several packs of strawberries under his jacket and it was the strawberries that had burst. Underneath the mess he was all right.

The noise of Mr Boyles' vehicle became familiar to me – often when I heard the *chug chug chug* of its engine it was the signal for me to light out and leave by the back door, on account of my chasing the Boyles daughters. If you could imagine following Mr Boyles into the house, with myself running away out the back, then immediately you'd get the full blast of the Boyles family way of life. In any room you went into there might be daylight and the weather coming in from some broken wall or ceiling. In the bath there'd be a vat of cider they'd made themselves. More often than not, everyone ate from the one pot in the middle of the table.

The Boyles family provided me with a set of brothers who dressed as Teddy Boys like I did when we went out to local dances. It was one of the fashions of the time – long coats, shiny trousers, crêpe-bottom shoes, a lick of hair teased over the forehead. There was a gang of us that went around – Albert Boyles, Bill Boyles, Tony Boyles, Charlie Prouse, Brian Tapp, Bill Hooten and me. And when you went into a dance with the Boyles brothers there were many who'd turn round and clear out straight away because there'd nearly always be a fight. If trouble started, the Boyles were sure to be involved, one way or another. In a dance at Dulverton once, three men picked on me in the toilet and I was knocked down. Bill Boyles came in and sorted all three of them out, sent them packing.

As well as the brothers, there were the Boyles girls. Doris was the one I went for – she had dark curly hair and a full face, very good-looking. It was because I was chasing Doris that I had to leave in a hurry when I heard that *chug chug chug* – her mum and dad were coming in their motorized shed. Once I pushed a bit of hardboard out the back window and jumped down. There was a big garden out there, and it was pitch dark. I ran this way and that, through the vegetable plot, stumbling over the broken bikes and rusting old machinery . . . and then I ran smack into a pit. I sank up to my knees. From the violent smell that immediately arose I knew I'd run into their toilet pit. They had outside toilets like most of us, but they emptied theirs into one spot rather than digging it into the vegetable garden. I'd fallen straight in it.

I dragged myself out and kept going. The stench was awful. I had bits of newspaper stuck to my legs – terrible, the worst escape ever. I went down to the river and rinsed myself off, so I was soaking wet when I got home. Still the smell hadn't gone. Mother realized something had happened and pestered me. She knew I'd run away from something and someone, as per usual.

Today if you go to that crossroads it's a very different place. The Boyles' house has been demolished and some way back from the crossroads, right around the same spot where I fell in the toilet pit, is the gracious white house built by my old headmistress, Mrs Bond. She was the one who asked me to put the trout back after I'd tickled it out of the river for her. She lives there still, over eighty years old.

My wife, Julie, remembers the first time we met, but I don't. It was very brief. She was thirteen years old. I was around eighteen and going out with a girl called Angela Kingdom, as it happened – no relation. It was on South Molton football field. We were introduced by Julie's friend Ruby Southcott. Julie was too young, so my gaze must have slid over her. But it marked the time I met the woman I was to marry and with whom I've now spent nearly fifty years.

The next time we met was when Julie was invited to come and stay with Ruby in Brayford, just down the hill from our house. She was nearly fourteen and suddenly I took to her. I started chasing her, just to walk in the woods, talk to her, and so on. But I was a cider man, and into fighting, and her family didn't want her to have anything to do with me.

They'd heard about other girls – God knows what. Maybe they'd been told about the girl I'd taken up to the top of the hayrick that stood in a barn halfway between home and the pub at Yard Down. Uncle Tony and Bill Maddox were making the three-mile walk back from the pub when they saw my bike outside the barn. They decided to interrupt and tease me, so in they came with their torches and started climbing up, calling and joking. I loosened a hay bale and sent it down. It hit Uncle Tony on the head and pushed him off the side of the rick. He fell to the floor – I can see him right now in my mind's eye, lying spreadeagled, the shaft of light from his torch beside him. I was lucky not to hurt him badly.

So Julie's family had maybe heard about that. I didn't sound like someone they could happily see their daughter with. And maybe they'd also heard about me taking that same walk back from the Yard Down pub, so drunk on cider that my uncles had to hold me under the arms on either side to stop me falling down. I told my two uncles, suddenly, about halfway down Beara Hill, that I had to stop. 'I gotta take a leak!' I sang. They turned me round and pointed me towards the hedge. As I got going, still singing, they thought it would be funny to let go of me. I pitched forwards into the hedge. It had just been cut by the hedge-trimmer and the sharpened prongs of two ferns went right into both nostrils and I bled like a pig. When they helped me back to my feet I was a terrible, drunken mess.

Had Julie's family heard that story?

Whatever they'd heard, it was enough to have them warn her off me. But I went on looking for her at dances, and so on. Outside the Assembly Rooms in South Molton she was taken away from me by her brother, Terry, and we had words about it. As he took her away they both had to watch me fall all the way down the stone steps outside, I was so drunk.

I refused to be put off. I managed to see her, one way or another. As the months went by and they had to spend so much time arguing with their own daughter, Julie's parents decided to change tack. They realized they were doing more harm than good. Their opposition made us more determined; it fanned the flames. Maybe if they let us see each other things would blow over quicker. Her mother invited me to their house.

The first time Julie came to our place, we ended up on the sofa, in the dark, like all courting couples. At half time, so to speak, Julie asked, 'What's that sound?' I listened, and heard a familiar clicking noise, along with the sound of the cricket that lived behind the chimney. I knew what to expect, but she didn't. We were both there in the darkness, on the couch. 'Dunno,' I said. 'Just go and put the light on.' She couldn't see the smile on my face. I could hear the tell-tale crunching noise as she crossed the room to the light switch. I couldn't even make her out it was so black. When she put the light on, there they were, crawling all over the floor – black beetles, or cockroaches. She screamed and jumped back on the couch and hiked her legs up.

The cockroaches always came out after dark. Mother would leave cucumber peelings to poison them, but they were too great in number. We'd grown used to them, but Julie was frightened. The couch was the safest place and she didn't dare run anywhere else. More's the pity – girls are more fun when they're running away.

We were all growing up, my sisters and I. They were out courting as well. But there was a strange hiccup around this time, for me. Two very pretty Church Army Sisters were sent to High Bray and took up residence in the vicarage caravan. These two seventeen-year-old girls were sent around from parish to parish to tempt people to church. If you stood in the little square of garden at the front of our house and threw a stone hard enough, it would fly over the lane, over the hedge, down over the strip of field, and it might just hit the caravan roof – so they had a good hold of my imagination; they weren't far away. I took to playing croquet with them. It sounds a bit odd, the idea of the local wild lad, always in fights or running away from bailiffs, policemen and farmers, playing croquet on the lawn like Lord so-and-so. But croquet is a wild game, anyone who's played it can tell you, and I liked how mean it made those two pretty girls.

During our croquet I found myself listening to all they said and taking their side in their beliefs and their values. I had been a choirboy, and Mother and Father were believers, so it wasn't a big jump for me to go the same way.

The upshot was that I came home and announced to anyone who'd listen, 'No swearing in this house from now on.'

The pipe must have dropped out of Father's mouth and Mother would have fainted at those words coming from the boy who'd effed and blinded his whole life.

'And no drinking of alcohol,' I added.

Like I say, Father had given up the cider by this time, but I drank it like it was water. This was a complete turnaround.

No one liked the new Johnny Kingdom. He was stuck-up. My sisters nicknamed me Brother John. They didn't like it one bit when I tried to convert them from their evil ways. They hatched a plan to push me off the wagon. They got my mates to take me up the road to Bratton Fleming, around four miles away. It was snowing, so it felt further. The first drink they gave me was lemonade, but they sneaked a shot of cider into it. They told everyone I was going to be a vicar so I could escape from the girls, which got my goat. The next lemonade had two shots of cider in it. By the time they'd finished I'd drunk fourteen pints of cider shandy, I was roaring drunk and all those pious thoughts had gone from my mind. Everyone was going on to a dance and I was going with them. Outside, the snow was lying thick on the ground and I took it into my head to roll a giant snowball. By the time we'd got to the dance hall, I'd rolled it so far that it was enormous, almost too heavy to lift. I was a strong lad and the cider had given me extra strength. I lifted this giant ball of snow above my head – like Atlas, I was – and they opened the doors to the dance hall. I staggered in. Joe Kiff, who was running the dance, came straight over. He was six feet four inches tall and he knew his event was in trouble now.

'Johnny Kingdom, do not throw that snowball!' he roared.

I couldn't exactly throw it because it was too heavy, but I certainly couldn't carry it any further. I dropped it in the middle of the dance floor – a huge pile of snow. Joe turned me round and ran me out of the dance hall and shut down the dance.

That was the last anyone saw of Brother John.

I suppose any story of a childhood and youth might end with moving out of the family home. But it wasn't so black and white for me. I finally said goodbye to my youth when I went to Hong Kong on National Service, but I'd stayed away from home once or twice before, if I'd had a tiff with Father.

On one of these occasions I went to stay with my eldest sister, Shirley. She'd married Derek Sharp, the man who'd helped Father with gravedigging. He was on the *Ark Royal* now, and so was away for long periods. They lived in a cottage down at Holewater, alongside the river. They had a son called Paul who was two at the time. I liked the change of living with my sister Shirley. And it wasn't too much further to walk to work, to Nott's Quarries.

Father's journey was the same as ever: out the house and into the little lane. Turn right towards the church. Fifty yards on, through the wrought-iron gate into the graveyard. A dozen paces over hallowed ground and down over the step in the bank, into the field beyond. Down along the river which we made a habit of taking the fish out of, then over the bridge and across the road, into the quarry to work.

Meanwhile, from my sister's house I was already by the river, so I'd walk downstream, to the same place of work, and join him there.

The only downside of staying with my sister was their son Paul's crying so much. My sister was fed up with it too. There didn't seem to be anything she could do to soothe him. Every night he cried. It was a good education for a young man, as to what it was like to have an infant in the house.

She took him to the doctor and he pointed out that

Paul was teething. It was part of growing up. I'd left my own house because of a tiff with Father, but I wasn't sure that this crying wasn't going to drive me right back again, or else somewhere else altogether. Coming up was the prospect of National Service. Of course, I could get work on a farm and that was a protected occupation, I wouldn't have to be called up. But I'd taken a fancy to the idea of this adventure.

Either side of his crying, Paul was a great lad. He had a special quality to him, even at that age, and with all the discomfort he was going through. We just wanted to hurry him up cutting his teeth. I have a picture of myself and him dating from this time. We're together in the graveyard, just in that corner near the wrought-iron gate, which Father and I crossed on our way to work, day after day, when we lived in the same house.

Shirley took Paul back to the doctor when the crying didn't stop. The doctor came back with the same report – Paul was teething. But there weren't the hectic marks on his cheeks. Shirley knew in her bones that this was something different and took him to a different doctor.

Paul was diagnosed with an inoperable brain tumour.

No one can face even looking at such sadness as losing a child; my sister Shirley and her husband had to suffer it. And that is when life tells you most harshly, that none of us has any idea, not a clue. Whatever's coming, whichever event is just around the corner, it's invisible, unheard, unknown.

Father and Mother helped nurse Paul as he grew more sick. For them, there must have been an echo back to their own first child, the one before Shirley, who was stillborn. Father had carried the tiny coffin for three miles through the snow. Now, with their first grandchild, they and Shirley and Derek all had to face another heartbreaking journey through a year of illness – and they knew there could only be the worst outcome. None of Paul's cries could be borne in hoping for improvement. Father, in particular, nursed Paul for many hours through his suffering.

Paul died aged three years old. Uncle Arthur dug his small grave, the spoil of earth splashed with his tears, no doubt. They chose as his last resting place that bottom corner of the graveyard which Father and I stepped across on our way to work. For the next forty years, every day, Father'd give a nod to Paul's grave and offer a prayer for the soul of that poor little lad whom he'd held and soothed for so long, before stepping over the bank and heading down the hill.

I still have the photograph of myself and Paul, standing almost on the exact same spot, as it turned out, where he was to be buried. If I were to stage this photograph again now, and put myself in the same picture, there I would be, sixty-seven years old at the time of writing, hair grown grey, having buried countless others,

myself. But I'd be standing on my own. Next to me, only two feet high – a gravestone in the shape of an open book, with three names on it, because my mother and father are buried in the same grave as little Paul. I put them in there myself, two of the last graves I dug before machines took over. On the left are the words 'Paul Derek Sharp, died 6 June 1959, aged three years, son of Derek and Shirley, brother of Tim'. On the right-hand page of the book is written 'Walter Kingdom, passed away 12 August 1996, aged 85 years, much loved husband and father and grampy. Also a loving mother, nanny and great gran, Joyce Catherine, reunited with Walter 18.9.2002, aged 86 years.' Underneath both pages run the words 'Never be forgotten'.

When I visit that churchyard now I can almost hear mine and Father's footsteps going past that spot. But no one makes that walk to work any more. A peaceful silence reigns.

PART TWO

At Her Majesty's pleasure

"He pointed a stubby finger at me and gave the usual challenge: 'See you in Nathan Road.'"

There was still National Service in 1959. Unless you were in a reserved occupation, you had to serve in the British Army for two years. Most young men my age escaped the call-up by working on farms, but I wanted to go; I fancied seeing the world. Father thought it was a good idea as well. We were in the kitchen; he leaned forward in his chair and pointed at me. 'You will meet your match,' he warned. I'd grown into a big fish in a small pond, and he saw the danger signs. 'It will make a man of you,' he said. 'Sort you out. Put you in your place.' Mother, on the other hand, didn't want me to go anywhere.

Julie said she'd wait for me; I promised I'd keep true to her.

I took the train to Oswestry, where I was to do twelve weeks' basic training. It was a big step. Neither I nor my family had ever gone anywhere. We thought if you went beyond Exeter you'd fall off the edge.

When we arrived at the barracks we got in line to pick up kit, mattress and bedding, which we carried to our billet. This was a dormitory of thirty or so beds in one long room.

The next I knew I was standing stark bollock naked in another queue, waiting for the doctor. The line shuffled forwards. The doctor grabbed my privates and said, '*Cough!* Right, on you go. Next!' It felt more like being a POW than a soldier.

Then came the injections. I tell you, in the army, try and get in the front of the queue for the needle. It's probably different now, but back then, after a dozen or so injections, the needle got blunt. They practically had to hammer it through the skin.

Next was the haircut. I had a duck's arse and a quiff like any respectable Teddy Boy, but in a couple of minutes it was down to a crew cut. I saw my ears for the first time in ages.

This was it: basic training. I thought the end of the world had come.

To be up at six wasn't a problem, training with the 25-pounders was all right, running twelve miles with full kit I could do. I was a first-class shot with the .303 rifle and the Sten gun, which wasn't surprising given the amount of practice I'd already had, hitting targets that actually moved. But it was the discipline and the square-bashing that got to me, and these guys who were smaller and younger and not as strong as you, who wore one stripe on their shoulders and who'd been to officer school. They wore me down until I was two inches small. When there was a locker inspection, everything had to be laid out with a measuring tape so the distance between objects was dead equal, but then an officer would pull it all out on the floor and shout, 'Bloody useless, Kingdom, do it again!' That was hard. The locker couldn't have been arranged straighter or neater; that wasn't the point. The idea was to break you down, to have you obey orders without question, even if those orders were rubbish.

This is what you needed just to clean your boots: candlewax, a heated spoon to press the pimples out of the leather on the toes, spit, black, polish brushes, cloth . . . We even had to polish the studs on the soles of the boots. It took hours of work with the wax and the spoon and the spit and the black and the polishing. Then the officer would pick them up, take one glance, throw them in the dirt and shout *'Bluddy filthy, Kingdom, clean 'em again!'*

I shaved until I was smooth as a baby's bum, and then went straight away on parade so not a single hair would have a chance to grow. The inspecting officer, born with a silver spoon up his arse, no doubt, grabbed me by the chin, wagged it violently as if he wanted to pull it off and shouted, *'Call that a shave, Kingdom, you useless hairy article!'* He quick-marched me to the billet and stood over me while I shaved again in front of the mirror – using cold water. Even as I shaved he kept me quick-marching on the spot. It was no good complaining or clocking him one; more and crueller punishments would come immediately.

It was hard not to kill someone. Or yourself. Father was right. I'd found my match. It wasn't someone bigger and stronger than me, it was the army itself and the Godawful amount of punishments that waited round every corner. I went from being a big fish in a small pond to a small fish in a big pond. I saw men crying with this treatment. I knuckled down. I kept going on the locker. I measured it more exactly. I put more shine on the boots. I drilled inch-perfect. The resistance was sucked out of me. Meanwhile Mother wrote to me twice a week, telling me to stick at it, that it wasn't for ever. Those letters helped me through; they were a life-line. They reminded me of what I'd been before, and what I knew I could be again, outside this pressure cooker.

Then it was time for the passing-out parade. If you failed at this, you'd have to do the whole thing again. I passed out OK – and so all of us were gathered in a room and asked which was our preferred posting.

Germany? Three-quarters of the lads put their hands up.

Hong Kong, anyone?

My hand was the only one in the air. Everyone looked

at me like I was mad. But I wanted to see the world. I didn't know that if you went to Hong Kong you only got one leave, whereas if you were posted in Europe you got two. I was stuck with it – but it was what I wanted: to go somewhere as different as possible.

I'd bashed out that square so many times and drilled so hard that I found myself among those chosen to go to Carlisle to parade in front of the Queen. We got a brief moment to go home before that, and I remember I took a cockroach (I called it a black beetle) off the kitchen floor and put it in a matchbox and took it all the way to Carlisle, to show the lads – they'd asked to see one.

We stood there in formation for three hours, waiting for Her Majesty. The crowd also waited. I was right at the back, and behind me, the other side of the rope, a small boy grabbed hold of the bayonet attached to my belt. I was on parade, stock still, and there was nothing I could do about it. He tugged at my bayonet some more. I'd need it later: one of the actions of the parade was to mount bayonets. It would be a disaster if I didn't have it. Whoever it was kept on tugging. He was going to have it off its hook any minute. So I kept my upper body dead still and kicked backwards, just once, with a highly polished boot. I heard a yelp, then silence.

It was just in time. The young Queen strolled along the line. She stood in front of me and looked me in the eye. I wonder what she was thinking at that exact moment. Are you reading this, Your Majesty? D'you remember me? I was thinking how pretty you were. I had my posting: Hong Kong, for the next nineteen months. Before I left the country I returned to High Bray wearing my army uniform, and felt rightfully proud. Mother burst into tears at the sight of me; Father didn't register much difference; he didn't like to show his feelings.

I met with Julie. She promised to write and to stay true to me. I promised the same to her. We'd wait for one another. It was only nineteen months. She was just fourteen years old; it was her birthday. I gave her a silver cross – and she still wears it today.

And then, very quickly, it was time to go. I went to Southampton to take up my berth on the SS *Oxfordshire*. Most of the other soldiers had family there to wave them off, but it was out of the question for mine to travel so far as Southampton. It seems strange now, with everyone going everywhere at the drop of a hat, but my family were rooted in one spot and it took a lot to move them off it.

It was tough on the *Oxfordshire*. We slept in chain beds, rows of us, and the floors were running with sick. None of us had been at sea before. We scrubbed decks, did our training, our drill, we shot balloons with our .303s out the back of the ship, but most of all we were sick. The ship was like one big gutter, running with the stuff. When the dinner bell went you'd collect your tray of food and there was an apple and an orange on it.

When you'd found your spot to eat, the apple and the orange would run up and down the tray, left to right and back again, and that was enough to make you sick again, even as you ate.

Around halfway, we found our sea legs. We were excited to see shark, and a whale. Sometimes flying fish landed on deck – they've got hard bony skulls, like they're wearing cycle helmets.

We reached the Suez Canal. It wasn't long since the trouble there and things were still tense. We were a large convoy of around thirty ships, but ours was the biggest. On the banks of the Canal men rode on camels, masks covering their faces, pointing their rifles at us. In the water lay the wrecks of ships that had been sunk during the crisis. You could have cut the air with a knife, but we passed through without incident.

We arrived at Hong Kong and were stationed in Kowloon, just across the water from Hong Kong itself, where the buildings rose so high it was unbelievable. Kowloon was the poor people's quarter of the city, in effect. The camp was a series of wooden huts on a slope, with a level tarmac parade ground for square-bashing. Suddenly we had to wear puttees, to protect our lower legs from snake bites.

Our first task was to round up hundreds of feral cats which had taken over the camp. They were caught in wire cages and put down by vets. I began to make a few friends. Joe Whitter was a little guy who had a tattoo of an eagle done on his chest; that tattoo was practically bigger than he was and looked like it was going to open its wings and carry him off. Brian Leatherby was bitten by a snake and was put in hospital in a cold room. Another man was bitten by a snake that came up through the toilet and he died.

Here's something that gives an idea of the level of humour in this place I'd ended up in: at the Waltzing Mathilda Inn they gave you a card as you came in through the door with the house rules printed on it. I can only give some of the less vulgar ones: 'NO LOUD FARTING. NO PLAYING WITH HOSTESS TITS. NO WIPING ARSE ON CURTAINS.'

At first we trained on 25-pound guns, but quickly moved on up to the bigger 55-pound guns which had a range of nine miles and took a 100-pound shell. Eight or ten of us worked each gun. There was one that exploded and killed three soldiers while I was there.

It was remarkable to see how the Chinese buried their dead. They were put in the ground in a coffin, as might happen to us. But then, some while later, when the corpse had rotted, the relatives came along, dug up the bones and counted them to make sure they had the right number. Then they polished them. I mean, really polished them, again and again, while saying prayers. It was an odd thing to see. Then the bones were put in a big ceramic urn and the top was sealed with cement. The urns were left above ground, positioned in straight lines. So, a family might have an area of ground with these lines of urns and they'd go up there on a Sunday and say prayers. It was strange, and it touched you. That was real devotion.

Twelve out of every seventy-five soldiers were taken on by the Regimental Police and I was one of them, on account of the fact that I was good at drill. We weren't the same as the Military Police, who arrested soldiers and brought them into the clink; us lot took them out again, on work detail. The work was digging trenches; the danger was the snakes that lived in the ground.

However, even with a uniform on and a job as a sort of policeman, it wasn't long before I was on the wrong side of the law. One night, there was a group of us out on the razzle on Nathan Road, which is where we all hung out. We rolled past a stall selling chicken. We were hungry but didn't want to pay for our food, not when there was more drink that had to be bought straight afterwards. The Chinaman who ran the stall was distracted by one of our group so that I could step in and lift out seven chicken legs, one for myself and each of my comrades. We were finishing off the chicken even as we barged into the Waltzing Mathilda Inn and ordered San Miguels. The next we knew, in came the police, truncheons swinging. We were cuffed, marched out and thrown into the back of a Black Maria. We admitted the

crime, paid for the chicken and were given our sentence –
fourteen days in jail.

There were five of us in one big cell. Two cigarettes
were allowed to each man every day: one at seven thirty
in the morning and the other at five thirty in the evening.
This wasn't enough, not by a long chalk. There were too
many hours to fill in between. Those hours dragged,
crawled along. We had to do something. My friend Brian
Leatherby was still on the outside and he agreed to
smuggle us in a length of string and a glove. When the
coast was clear, Brian tapped on the wall outside our cell
and we stood on each other's shoulders to reach the
window. We lowered the glove tied to the string, and
Brian filled it with cigarettes. We hauled the glove back in
and sat in our jail cell, smoking. That worked.

A guard came by. Quickly we stubbed out the cigarettes
in the little ventilation holes running along the bottom of
the wall. But one of them hadn't gone out. A finger of smoke
was curling up out of the hole and the guard was within
sight, sniffing the air. We couldn't reach down and stub it
out – it would give the game away. It was down to us to put
out that cigarette the only way a man can, by watering it.

When I was in the Regimental Police I was reported
for flipping a couple of cigarettes to a prisoner and as a
consequence of this I made an enemy of a Welsh boxer
called Davids. Anyway, he pointed a stubby finger at me
and gave the usual challenge: 'See you in Nathan Road.'

If I wasn't careful, this was going to hurt. He was a short, powerfully built man and a renowned boxer. Brian Leatherby gave me a piece of advice: get in early, catch him off his guard. If I could land the first blow then I'd stand a chance. If he tagged me first, I'd be on the floor for certain. Brian had an idea how to do this, and this is how it happened. When I next saw this man Davids, I tapped him on the shoulder and asked, 'What time, then, on the Nathan Road?' When he opened his mouth to answer, I hit him.

It didn't put him down. There was a full-scale fight, now, with a big circle of Chinamen and other soldiers shouting and hollering. But that first blow did count; in the end it did for him. I left him hanging off the railings, beaten. He wasn't going to be the one to put me in my place, after all.

It was on the Nathan Road, also, that you found the tattoo parlours. All the men had them done. Someone had a complete set of horse and hounds running down his back, with just the fox's tail coming out his backside as if it had just run down into its hole. There were those who went for the sort of thing likely to offend officers, like having *f*** off* written across your palm – so when you saluted, up went the insult. There was a Chinese man, I remember, who bet anyone a dollar they couldn't find a tattoo on his body. They'd crawl all over him, looking – under his armpits, on his scalp, everywhere.

You can imagine. Then they'd give up. He'd show them this tiny little swallow, right on the tip of his manhood, and he'd take his dollar. He made good money.

There was no anaesthetic used in the tattoo parlours on the Nathan Road. I sat on the stool and faced up to the Chinese tattoo artist with a bottle of San Miguel to hand. As he set to work I gritted my teeth and took a slug of beer – the drink was the anaesthetic.

The outline was the worst. He'd wipe the blood as it flowed off your skin, then lean forwards, inject more ink, carry on the line. I kept on gritting my teeth and drinking. The blood trickled. I lifted the bottle. More blood trickled. More drink. And so it went on. The Chinaman leaned over me, squinting. The sounds of the street came in from the open window. More drink, more blood wiped off. Afterwards I staggered out in a daze, pleased as Punch.

Before I went to Hong Kong I had one small tattoo on my arm – a pair of clasped hands with 'Mum and Dad' written across them. I came back with twenty-five all over my body. The biggest is a crucifix on my chest with an angel each side.

Back home again

"I was the exact same man I'd been when I'd left, only more so, and covered in tattoos.**"**

When the nineteen months were up I caught the boat back to England and was demobbed at Woolwich. We handed back the uniforms – boots and everything. But there was one thing I kept: my football shirt, from the Battleaxe team. We'd won the league out there and I was very proud of it. I had all my stuff in one big square case. I had to tie it up with rope after I dropped it 20 feet off a gangway and it split open.

I arrived back at South Molton station, the only person to step off the train and stand on the platform. It felt bizarre, so familiar and yet strange. A bus from Terraneous Tours took me to the town centre. I even knew the driver, Noel.

I rang home from the town square and asked for someone to come and pick me up. And there I stood, on home ground. There was the market in the middle of the square, same as always. The little wooden hut which collected the rent from stall holders. The Terraneous bus company, which ran the school bus. The café at the top of the square with the jukebox in it, owned by Claude Squires and his wife Maureen. All was exactly as it had been before, calm and quiet. People walked back and forth, same as ever. Some recognized me and exchanged greetings. It was a bright, hot day but I had on a big black coat because I didn't want anyone to see the tattoos on my arms.

I squared my shoulders and walked up North Street and straight into the pub nicknamed the Shed, or the Poacher's Paradise, as it was sometimes called, owned by Bill Mayne and his family. It was the place where men like me went. I walked up to the bar and ordered a pint of proper, west country rough cider.

'Hullo, Bill, I'm back again.'

'Hullo, Johnny.'

'How's Julie?' Julie was his daughter, the one I chased into the shed.

'She's very well, thank you.'

I drank my cider – cider that would rot your socks, as the saying went. Cider that you could not look through, was another saying. It went down without touching the sides. I was home. I climbed back into my old skin.

A few more jars of cider went the same way before Bill Yeo turned up to fetch me. He was going out with my sister Susan at that time. I was more than cheerful, I was well scammered when I got back to High Bray. There was the church at the top of the lane, and the same hedge where Father had shown me the cuckoo in the hedge sparrow's nest. Here was the row of houses, ours at the bottom end. The door opened. Mother took one look at me and burst into tears just like she'd done when I left. We all cried, in fact, except Father who as usual showed no emotion. No doubt he was looking to see if I'd met my match, if I'd been brought down a peg or two, if the army had made a man of me. All he'd have seen was that I was drunk on cider and reaching for the phone to chase Julie. I was the exact same man I'd been when I'd left, only more so, and covered in tattoos.

There was another reason for the excess of emotion in the Kingdom household that day. During my time in Hong Kong my three-year-old nephew, Paul Sharp, had died. Now, the day I'd come back from Hong Kong, his brother Timmy was born – and was straight into intensive care with a severe hare lip and cleft palate. I went to visit him at the hospital. It was heart-breaking. Where the top of his mouth should have been was nothing, an empty hole. This was a double cruelty on parents who'd suffered the death of their first born.

This time there was a happy ending. Surgeons made a new mouth for him. Today you'd never know it, there's only the shadow of a scar on his lip. He's a good man, is Tim Sharp, in his forties now.

I'd only brought back one gift from Hong Kong, and that was a music box for Julie. That gift, also, she's kept to this day. We spoke on the phone as soon as I got back. The next day I borrowed my sister's bike and cycled over to Grilstone Cottage, near South Molton, where she lived with her family. Her dad was farm bailiff for Captain Booth. It was a very hot day again but I still kept that black coat on. I wasn't ready to show those tattoos. It wasn't Julie I was worried about – there was a good chance she'd like them. No, it was her parents. They didn't want the likes of me, the local wild man, for their fifteen-year-old daughter. Especially not her father, Mr Carter. Coming back from the army covered in tattoos wasn't going to help my case.

When Julie and I clapped eyes on each other, it was just the same between us. She'd written to me during my time in Hong Kong saying she wanted to break it off because she wanted to be free to run with other people, and I'd agreed, but now that I was back we picked up where we'd left off.

I had no money, of course. I rode back and forth to see Julie on my sister's bicycle without any lights, always coming home in the dark, by moonlight if I was lucky, keeping one eye out for the police. Pedalling by the quarry one night I saw a car parked in a layby, its side lights on. I stood up on the pedals and put on a spurt to get past it without being caught, but an arm came out from in front of the car and caught me by the collar. It was like in a cartoon: the bike flew on without me. I was stopped dead by the long arm of the law, literally. It was Police Constable Walters. I can remember his words to this day, the classic line, 'Where d'you think you're going?' I could have answered him – 'Just back from two years' service for my country, with no money. What about you?' I was angry when he bothered to report me. There was a court case held, for heaven's sake. I refused to attend. Mother wrote a letter on my behalf; she explained I'd come out of the services and couldn't afford lights for the bike, which wasn't even mine – I'd borrowed it. None the less they fined me ten shillings. It still makes me angry to think about it. What a waste of time and public money.

The court case wouldn't help me win over Julie's family, either. I had my work cut out even more now. She wanted to be with me as much as I wanted to be with her, but this family of hers was frowning at me. Her brother Terry was coming round; he'd seen that although I wasn't as law-abiding as they might have liked I wasn't going to harm his sister. But the parents – they'd heard of the other girls and about the fights and the poaching. Big alarm bells rang in their heads at the mention of my name, even.

As it happened, being summer, it was the picnic season. The Carters were big fans of the picnic. They did it properly with rugs and Thermoses and even folding chairs carried out to favourite spots. Often they'd pick a high point, like the top of Porlock Hill, somewhere with a fine view, maybe of the sea or looking out over the purple haze of Exmoor's big rolling hills and steep wooded valleys. Or they'd go to famous beauty spots like Landacre Bridge or Tarr Steps. There'd be up to twenty-five people on these excursions which meant they could put together a good cricket match, as well. This summer there were several such outings along the riverbank. Now, the riverbank is my territory – it's where I can shine. I knew every sunny spot, all the best pools for swimming and paddling. One of those times we went to Brayley Bridge, a narrow little hump-backed, stone-built crossing. We headed downstream a ways, to find a big corner of the river there, with the firs coming down to the bank on one side and an open field on the other, where there was a deep pit for swimming. The sun was bright and hot. The picnic rugs were thrown out on the dry grass. The water was as clear as gin. We disturbed a salmon; it moved over to the bank to hide. I could see his tail just looking out from the weed. I always carried a fox wire with me, and I knelt in the water and carefully, slowly, put my hand down in the weed and tickled him until I could slip the wire noose around his tail. Then I pulled it tight and lifted a 10-pound salmon out of the water. Abracadabra.

Everyone knows how much a woman likes a magic trick. Mrs Carter, Julie's mother, began to like me a bit, and I liked her. We started to get on.

The picnic season continued. I became a part of that scene, even to the extent that suddenly a double burner was brought along to the picnic up at Landacre Bridge, up on the moors. There were seven of us. We found a quiet spot, upstream from the place the visitors went, and I tickled seven lovely trout, gutted them, heads off, washed them in the river – then we cooked them and ate them. I began to be appreciated for my talents, you might say. Perhaps Julie wouldn't be too badly off, hanging out with me.

Eventually I turned her father around, too. I went with a poaching gang up on the moors and brought him back a good piece of salmon. As a farm bailiff he was on the other side of the fence from me. It was his job to run a gang of workers on Captain Booth's farm and any one of them would see me off, if they saw me near their land. But after he'd tucked away this salmon he put his knife and fork together and he pushed away his plate and he said – I can remember the exact words – 'That was a bit moreish, John.'

He didn't quite smile, but nearly. I grinned at him. That was the first sign of approval I'd had. I started to call him 'Jim' instead of 'Mr Carter'.

Sure enough, from that point it began to look easier for Julie and me. There's nothing like feeding a girl well to win her family over.

And, by God, back in those years there were plenty

of salmon. The rivers ran with them. There was a gang that went out once by Landacre Bridge and they took nine in one session. I put together my own gang and we went out to see if we could top that. We were after ten. We went out the next night with a light and a gaffe. We got seven, then eight, then nine – so we'd matched the other gang's catch. But we couldn't get the tenth, not for the life of us. It was deep in November and it began to snow heavily. Eventually we had to call off our search for that tenth fish and head back up the hill to the van – a grey mini-van which belonged to one of us. You could hardly see it in the blizzard. There was no way we were going anywhere. We scooped out a hole in a gutter filled with snow, put the fish in there and covered them over. Then we started to walk. When we got to Sandy Way, we were struggling through high drifts and couldn't see our hands in front of our faces. We stopped at a farmhouse and asked to stay the night. The farmer said no, but we could sleep in the cowshed if we wanted. That was kind of him.

We decided to press on and started walking again. One of our number walked on quicker and disappeared from sight. We ploughed on. Walking through deep snow is exhausting. Add to that a blizzard blowing you backwards, and it's much worse. After several miles we came across a huge drift that had blown over the road, and the wind had put this cowl, like a roof made of snow, over it.

In one corner, under this roof, I saw a black shape against the snow. I walked over and touched it – and it was our mate. He'd gone in under there to get out of the blizzard and he'd fallen asleep. We were only a mile from home. If I hadn't seen him I believe he would have died out there. We made it back – with ice on our moustaches and hair – but we still had to pick up our salmon and the van. Julie's brother Terry tried to get through with his breakdown truck but didn't make it.

Five days later, the snow still lay thickly. We made a bet with the owner of the van: if he could get his vehicle out of there then he could keep all the salmon. He rang to say he'd done just that. The salmon were fine – still frozen. Thank you very much, he said.

We had such fun and games with our fishing. Fred Thorne, who married my cousin Pam, was so good at tickling trout that sometimes he'd have one in each hand. We had a catch of seven trout once, at Brayford, when a fisherman with a rod and line happened to come along. 'What d'you think you're doing?' he asked.

'Fishing, sir,' I said. 'Why?'

'Are you aware that you are poaching?'

'No, sir.'

'Let me tell you something. These fish belong to me. I own the fishing rights along this river.'

'Very sorry, sir. Can you tell us where your fishing rights start?'

'I own as far as the bridge.'

'Very good, sir, then we'll go below the bridge, and we won't be poaching your fish.'

He had a stunned look on his face, at the sight of us taking his seven trout, far more than he had, and we'd caught them without a rod, or a line, or a net, or a bag of tackle, or a licence, or any fishing rights.

I always kept a wire inside my trunks in summertime, while we played around and picnicked by the river. I got the wire around a salmon's tail once, when he took off and the cord attached to the snare broke. That salmon was gone, out of sight with just two swishes of his tail. We searched high and low for him. We'd recognize him for sure because he'd still be wearing my snare and the little bit of cord hanging off the end. But we couldn't find him. The next weekend we went back to the same spot and looked again. There were plenty of visitors around, but as far as they were concerned we were a group of young men larking about in the water. You might say that our brightly coloured swimming trunks and gym shoes were a kind of camouflage – we looked like them, we fitted in.

Sure enough we found the salmon, 200 yards upstream. He couldn't hide very well – the tell-tale cord drifted back from the stone he was under. There were visitors close by – I had to be careful not to be seen. I pretended to be swimming and edged nearer. Carefully

I tied another length of cord to the bit that was poking out from beneath the stone. Then I waited until the visitors were looking the other way and in one quick movement hauled out the salmon, killed and bagged it and we were on our way. The visitors hadn't seen a thing.

It was the complete opposite on another river, in a different year, when the visitors saw everything. A gang of us were carrying our catch home, wading across the river at a point where it wasn't very deep but it was wide, when the bag broke and all our fish were carried downstream, floating belly up. We hollered and shouted and splashed about, trying to get them back. The visitors laughed; they could see exactly what was going on.

There was one particular salmon that was the talk of poachers and fishermen alike back in those years. It was to be found in the Barle river which runs from Brendon Two Gates and heads south-east before joining the Exe. This cock fish was so crafty, but we'd all seen him, in a deep pit just a few hundred yards below a wooden foot-bridge not far from Tarr Steps. He was a monster, everyone agreed. He went back and forth between the pit and the wooden bridge, where he liked to hide under a patch of weed. But no one could catch him. I went out there and took a look-out with me so I could concentrate. I walked downstream from the bridge to the pit which was just out of sight past the bend – a stretch maybe 25 feet long, very still water, with a big clay bank on one side, where sandmartins and kingfishers nested. Trees grew on this side of the bank, whereas on the other side was a clear open field. I had my snare, and the cord was tied to my wrist.

Let's skip over the amount of time waiting, and watching, and move straight to when I saw him. There he was, hiding in the deepest part of this pit, where the water was four feet deep. There was no way I could reach it. So I held my breath and went underwater. I opened my eyes. The water was clear and cold and I could see this fish tail poking out from under a big stone. I had to move slowly, but there was only a certain amount of time available.

I pulled myself down near him, my lungs fit to burst. But I managed to slip the wire over the end of his tail. As soon as he felt me, that fish bolted. I'm not joking; this was an 18-pound male and he dragged me through the water, literally. Of course I had him, but it's not something you forget, being towed around a pit like you were being taken water-skiing. The power was incredible, and it's not surprising when you look at how salmon have to jump up weirs, and so on. Of course it wasn't long, just a few yards, until I found my feet on the river bottom and had my head out, gasping for air, and I hauled him on to the bank. What a lovely salmon that was. I was pleased as Punch.

Of course, people noticed he'd gone. 'Oh, really?' I'd

say when I was told. 'Someone had 'un?' From the glint in my eye, they knew.

So there was plenty of salmon, in those days, that I could pass to Jim, Julie's father. He'd said that salmon was 'a bit moreish' and so I brought him more. And the more he nibbled on the salmon, the more he looked on me with a kind eye. And that meant that Mrs Carter could afford to like me better, as well. In fact, fast forward a few years, when I was married to Julie and we had two baby sons, and my mother-in-law was with me when I caught a couple of salmon during one of our picnics. As we walked back she carried one in her towel, while I had the other draped around my neck. We were strolling along the river-bank, both of us poaching, more or less. She'd joined my side. Right on cue the water bailiff walked past. 'Good afternoon,' he said politely to us, the middle-aged lady and the young man walking in the sunshine. There was no sign of a gaffe or a stabber or even a rod and line, nothing to cause him any suspicion whatsoever. He just happened to miss two bloody great salmon, one being worn, clear as day, like a scarf.

There was still plenty that I kept from the Carter family, though. They didn't like me shooting deer. That was beyond the pale as far as they were concerned. Taking fish out of the river with your bare hands for a picnic feast was one thing. To go out with a gun and shoot deer was another. It went against the work he did as a farm bailiff, for one thing. Also, after he'd stopped work as farm bailiff, Jim worked in the butcher's shop in South Molton, and those of us who went around unofficially supplying venison to the general population were no doubt cutting into the butchers' trade. So he was always telling me not to shoot deer. He was worried I'd get into trouble and he was worried for his daughter, too.

It was Uncle Arthur who'd started me off on my education with guns. I used to watch him, when I was a child, making rifle slugs for his shotgun. He'd cut out a lump of lead and roll it into a ball. He'd shape it again and again, then he'd open the shotgun across his knee and drop the lead ball down the barrel. Perhaps it would be a fraction too big, or it would be too small and not fit the barrel snugly. He'd whittle away and smooth the lead until it was perfect, and he'd keep on trying the round ball in that barrel until it would roll down sweetly, just touching the sides. The slight twist he cut into it meant it would spin round as it came out – a rifle slug, but for a shotgun. Then he'd take a conventional twelve-bore cartridge, lever open the top and remove the lead shot. In its place he'd put the one big slug he'd made, then he'd seal up the cartridge again.

In effect he'd turned a twelve-bore into an elephant gun.

I was with Uncle Arthur once when he shot a stag in Beara Wood with one of these slugs, from around 45

yards. The stag was killed instantly and we took it home. But then a week or so later I happened to be going up the same valley with someone else; I was helping this gentleman look for antlers. We came across a dead stag lying there, quite near to the spot where Uncle Arthur had shot his. The man I was with was interested in these antlers, so I lifted the head – he had a fine set of points and we were going to set about cutting them off when something dropped out of the stag. I picked it up and recognized it immediately. It was Uncle Arthur's slug. It must have gone right through the first stag and killed this one as well.

'What's that?' he asked.

'I don't know,' I lied.

I showed it to him. 'That type of slug is illegal, isn't it?' asked my companion. 'Yes,' I replied. 'I believe you have to have a special kind of licence for it.' I slipped it into my pocket and took it home. At that time Uncle Arthur lived next door to us, after the White family had moved out, so when I got home I ran straight over. 'I got a present for you,' I told him. I put the slug on the table. 'That bullet killed two.'

So I was shooting stag from time to time. The venison would be butchered in the outhouse round the back, up towards where the vegetable gardens were, and the meat distributed to family and friends. However, as I said, I kept these activities secret from Julie's family.

Even as time went on, I only told her brother. He and I would become the best of friends. He would eventually own and run the garage in South Molton, while his father – Julie's father – worked in the butcher's shop, after he'd retired as farm bailiff. And the butcher's shop was right next door to the garage. Now imagine, here I came, round the back of this row of shops in South Molton, just as it was getting dark, carrying a quarter of a hind over my shoulder. I was taking it into the back of the garage, into Terry's place. I forget if it was for him or for someone he knew, but what I do remember is that on no account could I let Jim see me carrying that hindquarter over my shoulder around South Molton. But he was working right next door. I was sliding past, in under his nose.

Then my worst fear happened. I heard Jim's voice. I stopped dead. I could see the back of the butcher's shop, the door open and Jim's figure standing there.

I couldn't stay where I was, out in the open. I had to duck down and press on. I dashed into the back of Terry's garage, hoping that Jim wouldn't see me. I ran full pelt into the workshop area, the quarter section of hind bouncing on my shoulder.

Unfortunately, as I ran across the workshop floor – dodging tyres and hydraulic jacks, and so on – I put one foot straight into the inspection pit. A drop of five feet suddenly opened up beneath me. I was thrown sideways violently and I broke two ribs against the opposite side before I fell in. And somehow on the way through that workshop I dented someone's new car that was waiting there, as well. But I got out of the pit and kept going, somehow. I didn't stop until I'd hidden that quarter of stag at Terry's and got myself clear. There wasn't much that could stop me from running away.

So I never told Jim about shooting deer, not if I could help it, during all the long years I knew him.

The Carters did start to warm to me, but there was still plenty to put Jim off, as far as my being a prospective son-in-law was concerned. I rode a motorbike – that was another thing. At the time there was a new way of buying vehicles and household goods – hire purchase. The HP was the devil in disguise for me; I've given in to its temptations all my life and have only just got rid of it. But then it meant I could buy a fantastic motorbike, a 197 James. One night I was drinking in the pub up at Yard Down with Uncle Tony and Uncle Harry. Harry was an enormous man with a curly ginger beard which covered his face and grew down as far as his chest. He was comical and enjoyed his own jokes as much as everyone else's. He liked to tease people on market day. For instance, someone would ask him, 'What time is it, Harry?'

'Oh, hold on,' he'd say, and he'd start pulling at this chain in his waistcoat pocket, and he'd pull more and more chain out, and still more, until there was so much chain spooling out of that pocket that it would hit the floor, and on the end of the chain would be this tiny little watch. The next time, the next market day, someone would ask him again, 'What's the time, Harry?'

'Oh, hold on,' he'd say and he'd go to that same waist-coat pocket and start pulling at the chain, and this time there'd be the same length of chain, but something the size of a grandfather clock on the end of it. Harry was someone who worked on his humour, and all the time he kept up this patter, making everyone laugh. But he was just as quick to get angry. He was the sort of man you just had to stir up, one way or the other. Uncle Tony, on the other hand, had a slighter build, and he was a kinder, more gentle type.

Anyway, there was a whole gang of us in the Poltimore Arms up at Yard Down that evening, having a high old time and getting on the outside of a fair amount of cider. We spilled out of the pub around eleven-thirty at night to find our way home. Tony and Harry staggered over to their Austin 7 box car. By the time they were fumbling at the door handles I'd already started the James and was skidding around them in circles. I can picture Harry's red face now, beneath all that beard, shouting that I was making him mad, that I was to go on ahead. There was no way he was going before me; he was scared I'd run into the back of him. There wasn't much doubt in his mind that I was going to fall off my bike that evening. So I took off. I was long gone before they even managed to turn.

Beara Hill was on our way home. It's very steep, maybe one in five, and of course the one thing you're thinking is not to fall off. The cold air and the speed has a way of sobering you up, but on a hill like that if the front wheel of a motorbike hits the gravel in the middle of the lane, or the dirt at the sides, when you're braking hard, then you're gone. I was riding with all the courage that a few pints of cider can give.

I flew down safe and sound. No trouble.

Then I thought of something that would be really funny. This would get my uncles going. If they were expecting me to have an accident and fall off, let them see exactly that. It would scare the shits out of them.

Halfway down Beara Hill I pulled up. The James 197 had two butterfly nuts which tightened the headlamp and it was a matter of seconds to loosen them and aim the headlight up in the air. I jumped off and pushed the bike to the side of the road and leaned it into the hedge. The headlight lit up the overhanging trees on the other side of the road. They'd see it a mile away. The motorbike looked like it had just landed there. I walked a few yards further down the road and judged where I thought I would have landed if I'd fallen off. There I lay, in the gutter, any old how.

I waited, listening for the grumble of Uncle Harry's Austin 7 approaching. I could see its headlights coming down Beara Hill. I closed my eyes and let my jaw hang open, playing dead. I sensed the headlights on me. The engine got louder and I heard shouts from inside the car and the tyres skidding. Then came the shock as the Austin 7 ran me over. First the front wheel and then the back wheel went over my knee. *Thump-thump*. I didn't realize, but I'd left that leg hanging out in the middle of the road. There wasn't a lot of pain – maybe it was the amount of drink in me. I saw the car slew to a halt further down the road with Uncle Tony fighting to climb out. He stood there and he bellowed into the darkness, *'We bluddy killed the bugger!'*

Meanwhile, the only way to find out if the leg was broken was to try and stand on it. I got to my feet and limped over to the bike. I wasn't going to let them catch me. I pushed the headlamp straight, kicked the Villiers two-stroke engine into life and took off. I could hear Tony's shouts behind me: he was going to do this, he was going to do that, he was going to kill me.

I got home all right. I was too full of cider to worry much about my injuries, I just fell into bed and slept. During the night my leg swelled up and turned a horrible colour. I went to work the next morning at the quarry, and showed everyone where the tyre marks of the Austin 7 had literally printed on my skin. We had to dig out a chip of gravel which had been banged in. By this time Tony and Harry could see the joke. After all, they'd had the last laugh. Serve the bugger right, they said.

Winning the hand of Julie Carter

"She just had to be told, a little bit. She didn't want to give in too easily.**"**

Despite all this reckless behaviour I was still on course to win Julie. And I was pushing to go one step further. I didn't just want to go out with this girl, I wanted to marry her. I had to have her for my wife, and, as I saw it, her family was the only thing that might stop me.

The Carters often went down to Exmouth, where Julie's mum came from. Originally, she was Doris Vaughan, and her family had been newsagents there. They'd moved to Dulverton after the war, and from there to Grilstone, but they still liked to go back and visit Exmouth. They'd drive to Eggesford station and take the train, and sometimes I went with them.

It was when I was in the back of the car with Jim Carter, about to take such a journey, that I asked him if I could marry his daughter. I remember I chose a time when it was a bit gloomy, the light levels were low, he couldn't see my bloodshot eyes and skinned knuckles too well, he wouldn't notice the snare sticking out of my pocket and the shotgun folded up in my coat, so to speak. My tattoos were certainly well covered up. I can remember him peering at me through the gloom. He was humming and hahhing. He must have been on the rack. I've no doubt he didn't want to say yes, but how could he say no? If I had to guess, I'd say his preferred answer would have been, 'How about run around with her for a bit until someone better comes along? Now pass the salmon, John.'

At the end of the car journey we were joining the rest of the family, and Julie would be there. He had to give an answer, yes or no.

I waited. We turned into Eggesford station. He had to say, now. Which was it?

'Yes,' he said, just as we pulled up in the car park, 'all right, you can marry her.' I leapt out of the car, pleased as anything, and went straight to Julie. 'We're getting engaged,' I crowed, without so much as a by-your-leave. She was another creature I'd caught. I was proud. I'd got exactly what I wanted – a 'yes' off Mr Carter. But it was hardly the romantic approach.

'I'm not sure about that,' said Julie.

The world stopped. Julie was going to turn me down? This was a double turnaround all right – Julie saying no and her father saying yes. It was enough to confuse any man. 'Well, I'm telling you,' I said to Julie, 'we are, we're getting engaged.' I knew she wanted to,

really. She just had to be told, a little bit. She didn't want to give in too easily. She'd wanted a more romantic moment and I wish I'd given it, but there was romance just in the amount of need I had to marry her, and to get on with it – no time-wasters please.

Julie took me on. She said yes. I was twenty-four; she was eighteen. The year was 1963.

I was going to get the girl I wanted, after all. When I told Father he looked at me – I could tell he was wondering what on earth it was going to be that would teach me a lesson, bring me down a peg or two, give me the experience to make a man of me.

We were married in Bishop's Nympton, the parish where Julie's parents lived. It was filmed by Tony Linders, quarry foreman, who was also my best man, but the film has been lost, unfortunately. It was quite a big wedding, around eighty people or so, but it was a quiet and peaceful affair, and we happily gave our vows. Perhaps it was so quiet because of Father's illness. He'd been taken to hospital with a thrombosis in his leg. It's not difficult to see why he'd got one. At the quarry he worked a lot of the time with drills, the stone dust blowing up so that he was white all over his face and hair, where his hat didn't sit. When he took a break from that, it was to light up his pipe. And if he wasn't smoking a pipe then he was inhaling snuff. The only surprise was that it didn't happen sooner. I myself started smoking cigarettes when I was fourteen.

Players No 6. I'd collected so many tokens by now that we traded them in for an ironing board, right about this time, just before we were married. We still have that same ironing board today, over forty years later.

Anyway, Julie and I visited Father in hospital a few times. The doctor had told him he must give up smoking and take no more snuff. Julie and I approached his hospital bed. 'How are you?' I asked. It was cruel to see him lying there, his strength taken away, grey and ill. 'Not too bad,' he replied, and he had this odd smile on his face. I noticed a tell-tale brown stain on the front of his pyjama shirt. 'I hope you didn't take any snuff,' I said.

'No,' he replied.

'You sure?' I went on.

'I'm sure,' he said.

I pointed at his front. 'So what's that brown stuff on your pyjamas, then?'

'Well . . . my backside is brown, but I'm not pushing snuff up there, am I?' He looked at me and Julie, and after a bit he smiled slowly.

Julie was so shocked at what she'd heard that it took her a while before she started to laugh, but then she couldn't stop. Looking back, making a pretty girl laugh so much in a gloomy old hospital must have been a good tonic for him.

The sad part was that he could hardly walk at our wedding, barely move across the ground. We were all worried; I wish someone could have told us he'd live to eighty-six years old, stone dust and pipe smoke and snuff and all. There was plenty of life left in him. In fact, the antics of both he and an uncle of mine would, in the future, be described in a newspaper headline, 'GRAND-DADS CAUGHT POACHING TROUT'. He and this uncle, who shall remain nameless, were down at Holewater, helping themselves to a few trout, when someone reported them. Father was seventy-four, the uncle was fifty-nine. They were returning home, walking along carrying a bucket on a stick with the trout in there – a couple of harmless old men, it would look like. A bit further up the road a car was parked. They didn't think anything of it. When they drew near, someone got out of the car and announced himself. He was the water bailiff. He approached the two granddads and asked to see in the bucket. They pushed him away but he was deter-mined to have a look. So my uncle headbutted him and broke his teeth, and Father threatened him with a stick. These were two old guys with some kick left in them, for sure. The water bailiff grabbed the bucket and ran off with it. That was his evidence. There was a big legal battle, because they denied everything. My uncle stood up in court, cupped his ear and said, 'What? What? I can't hear you, sir, I can't hear you.' So he was given a spot right under the judge's bench. Still he put his hand behind his ear, 'Can't hear you, can't hear you.' Minutes afterwards they caught him talking in the cloakroom, his hearing perfectly all right. It was like something out of *Last of the Summer Wine*. The same few tiddly little trout – the evidence – were brought out from the freezer every time the court needed to look at them. My nephew Tim Sharp and I went along to watch the proceedings as they moved from one court to another. There was so much laughter, it was pure entertainment. We agreed that if Father got off we'd have a tattoo each to celebrate. My uncle was fined for breaking the bailiff's teeth, but Father got an absolute discharge. The judge looked down from underneath her wig – it was a woman this time – and told him to go home and put his feet up and not to be so silly. It was the laugh of the village for ages. We got our tattoos, me and Tim. He had one with his missus's name on it. Mine was a heart with flowers and an arrow through it, and Julie's name. But this was decades ahead of us when we first got married, and Father was so ill.

Julie and I went for our honeymoon to Plymouth Hoe, by train from Barnstaple. When we reached the place we were going to stay, at around lunch time, we knocked at the door and this figure opened it and pointed us straight upstairs, without asking us our names or anything. It was as if he'd been told what to do. He hurried us to our bedroom, told us the dinner gong would sound at six, then shut the door. I remember that big *gonnnnggg* . . . like the Rank film credit at the cinema, calling us down.

When we came back from honeymoon we moved into a flat above the flower shop in South Molton. It was a street I already knew, as it happened, because my cousin Terry – not my brother-in-law Terry – lived in the top flat next door to the one we were going into, and my old teacher Percy Banham lived round the back. I still see Percy every now and again in the pub or in the streets of South Molton, retired now and over eighty years old, and he always wags his finger at me and says, 'I know what happened that day, and that was a very good thing you did.' He's remembering when Julie and I were walking past Terry's flat and saw smoke pouring out the window. I put my coat over my head and ran up into the smoke to check he and his wife weren't in. There was raw heat and smoke, but no one there. When I came back down the fire brigade was arriving.

We lived the first months of our married life in that flat in South Molton. It had one bedroom, a kitchen and eating room, and the bathroom was on the next landing up – we shared it with the flat upstairs. We couldn't afford a cooker but the landlord, John Brookes, was kind to us and broke his usual rules and bought us one. The flat had bright red vinyl on the floor and we were very proud of the new cupboard with the glass doors, which would now look like a classic piece of 1960s furniture.

I went round on a BSA Star with Julie on the back. It was a great bike, 350cc twin cylinders, red with chrome trim. That would be a classic, now, too. I did have one bad smash on it, though, a year or two on. It was one of the times I took Father on the pillion, up to his parents' place in Witheridge, and it was on Christmas Eve. I came home on my own the next morning and passed a pub called the Gidley Arms, near South Molton. It was a fairly straight road and I was travelling at round 50 mph, perhaps a bit more carefully than usual because it was snowing. A car came out of the entrance to the pub – I didn't stand a chance. I canted the bike over sideways and went into him, ripping his front bumper round so it pointed straight out like a spear. My knee opened up; you could see the bone underneath. I actually stayed on the bike for another 25 yards, but then I grabbed the front brake too hard and the bike threw me right up in the sky. It felt like I was hundreds of feet up. Flakes of snow fell in my open mouth – I can remember that, like it was in slow motion. I pitched down on the side of my head and I would have been killed if it weren't for my helmet – which had a great gash cut in it. I slid down the road fast, on my back with my legs in the air. I glimpsed the bike spinning like a top near a gateway. When I'd come to a halt the car driver ran over to me. I subsequently learned that his name was Mr Drumund. He was an enormous man. He picked me up like I was a baby and lifted me into the back seat of his car. He had his wife in the front seat with him. He passed me back a drink in a plastic cup, but the cup broke in my hand, I was shaking so much. In hospital it took fourteen stitches to close the wound over my kneecap. There was a court case over this incident and Mr Drumund pleaded guilty without hesitation. I was paid £1000 compensation from his insurance company. More to the point, he became a good friend. Years later, the cruellest thing happened: his son Jamie was killed in a motorbike accident. I dug the grave for him, not in a churchyard but on the lawn of the family home. Friendship Cross was the place where he'd been killed, and friendship was the right word for it, because attending that young man's funeral were friends on 280 motorbikes. They were parked for near enough a mile down the road. It was a very sad occasion, but to have so many attend the burial was incredible and a testament to what a nice young man he was.

But this was a little bit in the future. For now, I had just got married to Julie and we lived in the flat in South Molton. I worked in the quarry and Julie had a job in the shirt and collar factory along with fourteen other machinists including her friend Janet Setherton. The factory was down at the bottom of East Street in South Molton.

Three weeks after we moved in together I became very ill. I had had an early start at the quarry – I was up at four thirty in the morning, to be there at five. I was helping Ern Parker make tarmac. We used our own chippings to mix with the tar we bought in. I was walking up the metal stairs that led up to the tar plant when suddenly I doubled over with a tremendous pain in my stomach. I near enough toppled down that long metal stairway, it was so bad. When I reached the top I collapsed and was taken to hospital. It was a strangled appendix and apparently it had been touch and go. 'You are a lucky young man,' the surgeon told me. 'We were just in time.'

'Well, thank you,' I said.

'And I can also tell you that there's nothing at all wrong with the rest of your stomach.'

'How d'you mean?'

'Well, I had your stomach out on the table and I had a good old rummage around in it, and I can tell you it's all perfectly healthy.'

I was amazed. 'You can't do things like that with a man's stomach, have it out on the table and poke around in it,' I said – although God knows I'd taken out the stomachs of animals often enough.

'Well, I'm afraid we *do* do things like that,' replied the surgeon. 'You don't know what we get up to when you're on the table.'

Onwards and upwards, driving cars and shooting guns

"... the windows slid open and there'd be a gun barrel sticking out of each one."

had the wife I wanted, I had a well-paid job, and was making more money on the side from the gravedigging. I recently worked out roughly how many graves I've dug in my life and it must be near enough 3,000. It means you think about life in a different kind of way. To see people through death has given me a greater reverence than I otherwise would have had, I think.

I often shared the gravedigging back then with my brother-in-law Derek Sharp. Like Father before me, I took out the tilley lamp when the winter evenings drew in and we had to work in the dark. So we walked up to the church at High Bray, a stone's throw from where I'd been born, from where I'd grown up, and where my parents still lived. The old building was a dark block of shadow against the night sky. We settled the tilley lamp in a safe spot, close enough for us to see what we were doing. The first thing was to lay out our template, which gave us the size of the coffin, and then we'd assemble our tools: a Devon shovel, a twelve-prong stone fork with the handle shortened a bit to work in the confined space, a pickaxe, and a saw or chainsaw to cut through any thick roots we might come across. We also had a sledge-hammer to break up any big stones. Then we took off the clats and dug down, keeping to the dimensions of the template so the coffin would fit all the way to the bottom.

The deeper we went, the darker it got. The tilley lamp was shifted closer to the edge. The surrounding gravestones began to take on a ghostly air; they seemed to move wildly back and forth when you moved the lamp. Once when we were digging in the dark, Derek said that he was going in for his tea. Was that OK? We weren't far off finishing, so I didn't mind. 'You go ahead,' I replied.

It grew darker. I was left alone, digging away, up to my neck in this grave, surrounded by the long dead. After a bit I did start to mind that I was alone. Not because of the work, though. But here I was, cutting down through earth where men and women and children had been buried for hundreds of years.

It began to spook me. I tried to shrug it off, but couldn't. If I looked up over the edge of the grave the crooked tablets of stone standing in rows looked like an army of the dead, about to come to life. I could see my own breath, a ghostly cloud of white vapour shown up by the tilley lamp. I told myself to put my head down and keep on digging. That was the only way to stop those kinds of thoughts – get on with the bloody work and not give yourself the space to think of anything else. There was just the sound of the pick going into the earth, my breathing, the grunts as I lifted each spadeful out and tossed it up over the lip of the grave on to the heap of spoil.

Then I heard a noise, a sort of moan. Was it the breeze moving round the big old church, had the air caught against some sharp edge or blown in some nook or hollow . . . ?

I worked more quickly; I wanted to get out of there.

The noise came again. I looked around. The tilley lamp cast the nearest gravestones almost white, then increasingly shadowy towards the edge of the graveyard. Trees stood on the boundary wall – black, leafless silhouettes against the night sky.

There – it came again. It was like someone in pain. And a shape moved. I didn't even think about it, I leapt out of the grave, double-quick. There was no way I was going to be caught stuck in a deep hole in the ground by someone – or something . . .

A white shape swam across my line of sight, about four gravestones distant. I threw down the spade and clattered away from that grave just as fast as I could. I weaved in among the stones, down the path, through the wrought-iron gate, the devil at my heels. I ran the hundred yards down the road to Mother and Father's place, where I knew Derek had gone.

When I ran in, Derek was already laughing. It had all been a big joke played on me. It was why he'd gone early: to leave me by myself so that Uncle Tony could put a sheet over his head and spook me. It had worked, as well. Totally.

Julie and I were in the flat in South Molton for about six months. Then Bill Dart's grandpa, Tommy Dart, who was council bailiff, helped us through the whole business of getting a council house in Bishop's Nympton. He knew Julie's dad and put in a good word for us. And so it happened. We moved into the house in which we still live. The hedges were all overgrown and the back garden was a jungle of nettles. My father-in-law and I set to work and cleared them.

There was a general opinion, when we moved into Bishop's Nympton, that it was a bad day for the town. This was because there was already one poacher who lived here, and two of us living so close together looked dangerous. The local landowners didn't like it, and there were a lot of religious people as well who didn't want a man living among them who drank too much cider and took his shirt off in the dance halls and crashed his motor vehicles. None of them was wrong to have this opinion, as it happened, and I didn't object to the truth being held up in front of me. That's what I was, and how I lived. It made me happy, but it wasn't such good news for some of them.

We've been here for well over forty years. And we've made such good friends; I'd not have lived anywhere else. One of these friends was Ray Setherton – a brilliant bloke. He was sixteen or more years older than me, and had fought in the war. He'd suffered terrible injuries to his face – he'd been blown up and burned – and he underwent seventy operations. He'd been to hell and back, having his whole palate rebuilt using muscle from his arm. He only had one eye, so he used a glass one, and because of the damage to his face, this glass eye would quite often drop out and break, so he had to buy them two dozen at a time. He'd keep a box of eyes at home and dip into it when he needed another one. We'd go drinking together in my Ford Consul. At the pub down at Bish Mill he had his own seat with his name engraved on a brass plaque in the back of it. When it came to the time for him to visit the Gents, he'd pop his glass eye out and drop it in his pint of beer and say to it, 'You look after my pint, mind, I'm going for a slash.' The eye would sink to the bottom and stare up at you through the drink. He was a remarkable man, the funniest, the best, and he is sorely missed.

One night Ray Setherton and I were driving back from the Bish Mill and up over Selcombe Hill. Behind us came my cousin Philip, Uncle Tony's boy. We got up on to the level and his headlights were right up our backside. Ray said to me, 'Road's fairly wide here, let 'un pass, let 'un pass.' I agreed, 'OK, Ray.' Unfortunately I was already on the wrong side of the road, and so I steered further to the right and we drifted into a ditch. The car turned over and lay on its side. Ray and I were all jumbled on top of each other because we weren't wearing seat belts and the Consul had a bench front seat. Philip, driving along behind, sailed past without seeing us, didn't miss us one bit. He went straight on home, where he was surprised to hear from Julie that we hadn't arrived yet.

Meanwhile, Ray and I were trying to get out of the car. We had to climb up the bench seat, and push the door up over our heads. It was a heavy door. It wasn't easy, when you're laughing so much. Eventually we were sitting on the side of the car, letting ourselves down. We had to walk all the way home.

'What happened to you?' they asked.

'Went into the bluddy ditch and turned over. Didn't you see us?'

The next day my brother-in-law Terry sent Mike Warren out with the breakdown truck and tipped the Ford back up the right way. There wasn't a scratch on it.

It had gone over so gently, and the steel was that thick, and the ground so soft, there was no damage whatsoever; just a bit of mud to be wiped off and it was good as new.

Hire purchase meant that I could have the motorbike on tick and buy an old Morris 1000 van as well. I did fancy a Traveller, the one with the wooden chassis, but I couldn't afford it. The Morris 1000 was a great vehicle, though. We even took it swimming once. We headed up to Tarr Steps, a beautiful part of the moor. I had Julie in the front, eight months pregnant and big as a mountain. Two of my sisters – Rosalind and Thelma – were in the back of the van. It was September, a lovely autumn day, but there had been a great storm the day before. When we came up to the ford at Tarr Steps the traffic was all backed up. The scenery was as pretty as you could want; the weather was fine and sunny. Yet we had this hold-up. The long and short of it was that the water was too deep, they said, to drive across. 'Out the way,' I said. All that was needed was for someone to take a lead, show how it's done. We started out across the ford. The river was high, I'd admit that. It started to worry me just a little. Water came in through the van doors and started to flood us out. The next thing was, the engine gurgled and spluttered and died. The van was rocking gently and moving sideways. I noticed that all the other visitors were beginning to enjoy the spectacle from the safety of the giant stones that cross the river. They had their cameras out and were taking pictures. When we were bumping up against the stones, I wound down my window and shouted, 'You silly sods, don't bluddy stand there, come and get us out!' The water was filling the front of the van. Julie was trying to crawl into the back, which was difficult since she was as big as a house. The van was swimming, or scudding along the bottom of the river. It filled right up with water and it took eight full-sized men, wading in the river up to their waists, to push us out. When the poor old van was out the other side we could afford to laugh about it. It took me hours to dismantle and dry out all the bits of the engine – the plugs, the points, and so on – but eventually we put it back together and got it working again. It was a different type of day out altogether. I've always wanted to see one of the photographs those visitors took.

That van took some punishment, all right. We had a puncture once, it was the nearside front wheel, and it blew just as we were on the way back from Brayford. We'd no sooner pulled in than a mechanic employed by Nott's Quarries drove round the corner and helped us change the wheel. 'No problem,' he said. 'I'll jack that up for you.' And he did. He changed the wheel, let the car down off the jack and we all went home. You'd think that was a piece of good luck, a friendly mechanic turning up just when he was needed. We made our way back to Julie's parents' place at Grilstone. Just as you're coming up to the entrance there's a dip in the road. We were on our way down this slope when Julie pointed ahead of her and asked, 'Is that our wheel?' And it was. It had over-taken us, rolling ahead like it was more keen than we were on the whole visit. The van itself only noticed one of its wheels was missing when it came to the bottom of the slope and banged down on the hub. Julie was heavily pregnant with Craig, and she lurched over and squawked. I swore. The hub ploughed up the tarmac. But we all survived.

There was another incident with that van, in fact, and this time there was a casualty. Julie and I were driving home and as usual I had the .410 belonging to my father hidden behind the back seat. We passed by a disused quarry pit that I knew, and I pulled over.

'What are you doing?' asked Julie.

'Just getting us a pheasant for our tea,' I said and reached for where the gun was hidden. Julie had a go at me. She'd never have anything to do with killing anything and didn't want to be near me if I was. 'Don't, not in front of me!' she cried. We had words; I wanted a pheasant. The argument ended with me getting out the van and going into the quarry with the gun, and Julie staying in the van.

I can picture her now, head bowed, angry. 'All right, then,' I said to myself. 'Let's see.'

I went into the quarry and started walking through a stand of birch saplings and brambles growing close together. All of a sudden there was the characteristic *whush whush!* of pheasants' wings and its alarm call, *Chuck chuck chuck* . . . It was well up and flying by the time I had the gun on it. I fired. It spun, dead in the air, and went down – and it pitched smack on the windscreen of the van. Julie jumped out of her skin. She didn't know what was going on. She was frightened to death. There was blood and feathers everywhere. I came back out of the quarry to find her in a hell of a state. What act of God was it to have that bird land in front of her, right in the middle of that argument? You can imagine that I wasn't popular. I apologized over and over, but there was no undoing it. The whole episode had to pass by, for it to be all right between us again.

The other vehicle I had during these early years of my marriage was a black Austin 10. We called it the Hearse because it was a solid lump of a thing, black from top to toe, with dark, sliding windows. We'd go out poaching in that car. The best time was to wait for snow and ice, when there wouldn't be any police around. We'd take our guns and get in the car and drive round. When we got near to where the pheasants were being reared, the windows slid open and there'd be a gun barrel sticking out of each one.

We'd have ourselves a shooting party, like we were a bunch of gangsters. We'd chuck the pheasants in the boot, five or ten at a time. The only trace left behind would be blood on the snow, just like in *The Godfather*.

I can't resist just one more vehicle story – the Skoda in the cabbage patch.

I had some scrapes in my old Skoda. Back in those days there weren't the same worries over drinking and driving. We went to Bratton Fleming to celebrate a soldier's return from duty. We played darts, drank Red Barrow beer and rum-and-peps, and had a high old time. On the way home I was stroking the hedges a bit, I must confess. Coming down into Brayford there's a sharp left-hander on a hill, and I did slow down all right, but even so I had to allow the Skoda to run into the bank before I got round it, third time lucky. We swerved over the bridge, heading up to High Bray, when we suddenly realized that the car following us was not that of our drinking pals, but the police. It was something to do with the blue flashing lights that made us put two and two together. We were up near Farmer Tucker's place at this point, right next to where I was raised, so I knew every little trick round here. I flew down this rough cart track for about a quarter of a mile, but the police car followed. When we came up to the gateway at the other end I slid to a halt, put the car in reverse and spun round. The police car came to the same spot and stopped as well, but I had just enough of a gap –

if I put one wheel in the ditch – to fly past him. And I did. But he turned as well, and still he came after me. We were going like hell now, up the lane towards the church, cutting across the top of the village square and up the track the other side, out to the back gardens and the allotments. It was just like a country version of *Starsky and Hutch*. The Skoda ploughed into a cabbage bed and dug itself in. We were stuck. The law arrived, lights flashing, siren blaring. There was a tapping at my side window.

'What the f***ing hell's goin' *on*?' I asked the officer, as if it were all his fault.

'I think you'd better step out that car, Johnny Kingdom,' he replied. 'How much have you had to drink?'

'I had two pints of Red Barrow, sir, that's all.'

We moved to the comfort of the back seat of his panda car. 'Breathe into this, please.' He handed over the old-fashioned type of breathalyser. I blew into the pipe, just a tiny breath, a sip. I was very reluctant, if truth be told.

'You short of breath, Johnny?' the policeman asked. 'Well, that doesn't matter. It doesn't count, how much or how little you blow into it. It's either red or green, no way out of it. Red if you're over, green if you're under.'

That was me done for, then. There was no question. I was miles over the limit, out of sight.

The light turned green. It was hard not to laugh. There must have been something wrong with the machine. The gods were looking down on us. 'There you go!' I said, outraged. 'See? I told you, I only had two pints and that was a while ago. I got afraid because you were chasing me. If you start harassing innocent people all round the countryside late at night, you can't be surprised when they start running away, can you?'

'Are you getting back in that car?' asked the officer, pointing at the Skoda in the cabbage patch.

'No, your honour, I'm staying right here with me mum.'

When the police car had gone, we managed to get the Skoda out from among the cabbages and I drove home to Bishop's Nympton. I only hit the hedge twice more. I loved that breathalyser.

Life was good. I was stronger and fitter than ever. And the icing on the cake was the birth of our two sons, Stuart and Craig.

Stuart came first, and when he was close, any day now, there was hellish snow on Exmoor. I got worried we'd never get to the hospital. I called my in-laws and asked them to meet us at the top of the hill. They could bring a tractor from Grilstone to haul us out if we got stuck, and then we could stay at theirs until the snow was gone. When we got to the top, near the main road, the snow was so thick we couldn't see the signpost at the side of the road. So we ended up going down Selcombe Hill, the way we didn't want to go. At the bottom we met up with the tractor and they escorted us back to

Grilstone, where there was not one flake of snow, believe it or not.

A few days later Stuart still hadn't arrived. We took ourselves into the hospital and suddenly, on Friday 3 December, 1965, Julie was in business. She was taken off somewhere and I was left trying to catch up. I had to find out where they'd taken her. I went into a maternity ward and asked the other women, 'Where's my wife?' They pointed, 'That way, in the delivery room.' I walked straight in – didn't think about masks or anything like that – and I just got one glimpse of Julie with her legs in the air and the screams and all that, and, oh my God, I smartly turned straight back round again and walked out, went straight down to the car, got in, started it up, drove directly to the Poltimore Arms, ran inside and drank a whole bottle of port. What a coward I was! It wasn't the done thing in those days for men to be present at the birth of their children, but even so. Julie had a very difficult time of it, and when we got Stuart home he cried a lot with colic. All through the night, Julie tells me, I'd have him lying on my chest so she could sleep. Stuart turned out such a good lad.

Craig, my youngest, was born four years later, on 6 August 1969, and the time of his birth will always remind me of the night I shared a jail cell with a deer.

I was with a great mate of mine, a man I often went shooting with, usually rabbits or pheasants. On this occasion, though, we'd shot a deer. We even had permission from the farmer. I can't say I always had permission, by any means, but this time we did. It was going to be a lesson to me, in fact, always to get permission in writing.

Anyway, the deer was shot by my friend. It was an old stag. Its antlers had the brow points, the lowest ones, but the next ones up, the bay points, were missing. It had the next after that, the tray points, and two points on top. So we'd describe its head as 'brow, tray to a top'.

Together we hauled this old stag out of the cover and lifted it into the back of the Morris 1000 and shut the doors. We had the dealer already lined up; he was waiting in Barnstaple and he wanted to pay us £10 for this deer.

By the time we were on the road to Barnstaple it was maybe ten o'clock at night. Just past Aller Cross Garage a police bike came storming up behind, headlight blazing, blue light going round. I pulled into a layby and stopped. The police bike didn't come in behind me, he dived to a halt just by my door, as if he was expecting me to jump out and make a run for it. Anyone would think I'd robbed a bank. I wound down my window. 'Yes, officer?' I knew this one. We weren't exactly the best of friends.

'Johnny, your nearside tail light isn't burning.'

'Oh,' I said, 'let's have a look.' He parked his bike and I got out the van and walked round the back.

'There,' he said, pointing. I knelt down and wiped my hand across the glass. 'Well,' I said, 'look, it's only a bit of shit.' Sure enough a glimmer of red appeared. The Morris 1000 hasn't got the most sparkling rear lights at the best of times. 'There you go, right as rain,' I said, and made ready to be off.

'Hang on, Johnny,' he said. 'While you're here, let's see what's in the back.'

I was angry with him now. I opened the door faster than I should have and he bent his head in. Perhaps I shouldn't say that I wanted to kick his backside. No one should even think of doing such a thing. 'See? It's a bloody stag,' I shouted, 'are you happy now?' We glared at each other. 'You knew it was in there, and that's why you stopped me, but I've got permission to take it, so—'

'Enough!' he shouted back. 'I'm taking you in. Follow me.'

He mounted his police bike – the usual white Triumph with a full fairing – and he spun it round, kicking up the gravel, and headed back towards South Molton. I turned the van, effing and blinding, and followed him. All I wanted was to get this over with in short order so I could get back to my heavily pregnant wife. My friend in the passenger seat was keeping his head down, but he'd been seen; we were both in trouble. It was illegal to move dead stock at night, quite apart from anything else. It was a law that was specifically designed to stop poaching.

As we followed the police bike, for some reason my engine started missing. First of all I lost one cylinder, then two. We were crawling along. We lost sight of the police bike. I pulled over and tried to rev the engine and clear out the blockage or whatever it was. A minute later the Triumph came thundering back and skidded round like on a speedway circuit to end up alongside my window once again. 'Sorry, officer,' I said, 'she's missing on two cylinders.' I knew he wouldn't believe me.

'Any more funny business and you'll be in more trouble than you can know,' he said and tore off again. We limped along behind him to South Molton police station. It was around eleven o'clock on a Sunday evening by this time, and the pubs were kicking out. Everyone stopped to look. After all, any vehicle belonging to Johnny Kingdom parked outside the police station in the middle of the night, with a dead stag hanging out the back and the doors wide open, and a couple of officers circling round, was bound to excite comment. I won't say there wouldn't be a few pleased to see such a sight.

My only thought was for Julie. Had she gone into labour? I was anxious as hell. My partner in crime was taken upstairs; they separated us off for questioning. PC Easton was with me now and I was much happier. He was a brilliant bloke and we became good friends. His nickname was Bones. 'You know what you've got to do now?' he said.

'No, what?'

'Unload that stag and haul it up those steps into the station.'

'You are joking.'

'I am not joking.'

'That's a two man job, that is. It's a whole big stag in there. I can't do that by myself.'

'I'll help you, then.'

So Bones and I hauled this poor stag out the van and up the steps. It seemed like they were going to a lot of trouble for not much reason. It was my reputation that was to blame. I'd have been a feather in any policeman's hat around that area.

Together we dragged this stag into the police station. 'A few yards more,' he said and nodded at a cell, the door standing open. We dragged that deer into the cell and then he locked me in there with it – a deer I didn't actually shoot myself and that we had permission to take anyway. They took a statement off me and said they were going to check it against the one made by my friend. I prayed that he'd say the same as me – the truth – and then I could get out of here and back to Julie. I had terrible visions of her going into labour all by herself . . .

It was very, very cold that night and there was no heating in my police cell. I walked back and forth and flapped my arms round my chest. I could see my own

breath, it was so cold. The deer lay in the corner, dead as a doornail. I blew into my hands and paced up and down some more. It was freezing, it really was.

To make things worse, through the bars I could see Bones sitting up close to a nice tall stove, smoking a pipe and drinking tea.

Two or three hours passed like this. Eventually I called out to him, 'Could I have a drink?'

'Yes,' he replied. He came and unlocked my cell, and it was better than I could have thought. He not only gave me a drink but he let me out and put me beside the stove as well. I told him how worried I was, Julie being so heavily pregnant. At any moment she could go into labour. I had to get home quick.

Then my friend came down. They were letting him go but keeping me in still, because the statement I'd given was different from his. I didn't care what I said by this time; I'd do anything to get home. I made a new statement and I told them what they wanted to hear and they let me go. They kept our guns, and they kept the stag. As I left I said, 'We want that stag back, mind, that's our property, we know where it is.'

A case was brought against us by the police, and three weeks into that process Julie went into labour. We were at home and I didn't take much notice. I was sure that the birth would be some way off yet. 'It's going to be a long night, I'd better get some sleep,' I said, and I went to bed, believe it or not. The next thing I knew, Julie woke me up. 'We have to go to hospital, now.' Her tone of voice told me it was urgent. We were out the house like a rocket. Every two miles the pain was worse. We only just arrived at the hospital when Craig was born, right as rain. But if we'd left it any later he'd have been born in the van or on the steps of the hospital. He's a great lad, grown up now – a chip off the old block.

Seven weeks after Craig was born, Julie happened to be in South Molton when that same policeman came up to her and said, 'You can tell Johnny the case is over. He can come and pick up his guns.'

They hadn't got me. The prosecution collapsed, as it should have. I went down to the police station and said, 'Right, now it's my turn. I not only want my guns back, I want that deer as well.' It turned out that, following its night in the cell with me, the deer had been taken to a freezer over at Mr Gregory's factory. He ran an egg-packing plant nearby. They'd kept it in there as evidence. Then it had been moved to a freezer down in Barnstaple. The police reminded me not to pick it up after dark, which would be an offence. 'If you do,' they said, 'we'll book you again.'

'You rotten sods,' I said.

So we drove to Barnstaple and walked into that freezer and there was our stag, whole, in the corner, covered in ice and frost. It looked like one of Santa's reindeer had fallen out of the sky. So we took it out and tried to fit it in the back of the van. Of course it wouldn't go in; it was frozen solid and its head stuck out the back. We tied the van doors shut as well as we could and headed for home. That meant driving through South Molton, right through the square. You can imagine how good I felt about that. We took the stag to Bishop's Nympton, to my house, and put it on the lawn. We had to move fast because it was thawing out. We had to clean it up, make it ready. It took a bit of work with a knife and a chainsaw, but then I could go indoors and call that same dealer and say, 'Remember that stag you didn't get? Well, d'you still want it?'

'Yes, please.'

Back we went to Barnstaple. We got our £10 and the stag went for dog meat. What a load of fuss for nothing.

All this happened thirty-seven years ago, the year of my younger son Craig's birth. And today there are more deer shot than ever before.

Branching out on my own

"Everything I had I wanted,
and everything I wanted I had."

By now I'd worked for eleven years alongside Father at Nott's Quarries. I had an eye on being my own boss, earning better money, moving on and upwards. I had the idea that if I bought a chainsaw on HP I could fell big timber for piece work, and if I worked hard enough I'd do better for myself and my family. This I did, leaving Father behind to carry on as before. He would give a lifetime's work to the quarry, as it turned out.

We were paid so much a square foot to clear trees. It was hard work and we'd start at five in the morning if it was summer, to get the cool part of the day. We'd cut all week and burn the tops as we went along, sometimes the whole family helping. On Sundays we'd load up the lorries by hand; the timber was hauled up to Wales by road. I worked for any number of people over the years. We were paid 5p per square foot for straight felling, and 12p a square foot if we were burning the tops. Stuart, my eldest, started coming along and Julie would join us at weekends to help with the burning, and later Craig too. I'd always start the bonfire with a tyre with a drop of petrol in it; that never failed to kick it off, just like the ones we'd done on bonfire nights. I worked often with the Boyles family – Albert, Bill, Tony, my brother-in-law Martin, and Mike. They were the top men at tree work.

When Dutch Elm disease came along, Albert and I went all the way to Cornwall every day for three months, felling. Albert would be on the tractor, I'd climb the tree and put up the steel wire, then he'd call, 'Are you ready?' and back would come my answer, 'Not quite,' and he'd haul the tree back anyway. He worked at a pace, did Albert. He wasn't overly concerned as to how far clear I was. There were times I'd have to jump out of the tree as he was pulling it. That suited me; the money was for each piece of work and so the harder we worked the more we earned. He was a brilliant bloke, a big strong man, doing the right job for sure. I then employed a young man to help me, called Gary Setherton. He was a good laugh, maybe eighteen years old. The first job I took him on was near Crediton, on the Downs estate. They had a gardener called Tickle, if I remember rightly. Our task was to clear a cover of big oak trees, set quite close together. The first one I cut hung up – leaned against its neighbour. I felled another and that hung up, too. And the next. In the end there were five mature oaks, all hung up on the one tree. The amount of pressure on that tree must have been enormous. I called to Gary, 'Shout if you see anything moving.' I went in under those five trees and drilled the nose of the chainsaw into the centre of the trunk holding them up. Then I sliced through the thickest piece of root.

That tree went away quicker than anything I've ever seen – like a rocket. The five of them came down at once. It took all day to limb them out. It was a dramatic first day's work for Gary. He and his family run a building firm now. They're doing well.

I was at the top of my game in every way. I was earning good money – more than ever before, now that I was my own boss and could put in the hours necessary. I bought our house, for £10,900. I was fit and healthy. I'd won the hand in marriage of the prettiest girl in the west country. She had two strong boys running at her feet. I could put any amount of game or fish on the table to keep us fed. I was captain of the darts team, and I was manager of the local football B team. I could work from before the sun got up until after dark. I could hold my own with the cider, pint for pint, against anyone. I was in all the pubs and the dance halls. I'd fallen into most of the ditches in the area. I'd crashed a respectable number of cars and motorbikes. I had good friends around me – any time I wanted I could find a good laugh and a good night out. I even had a few enemies to keep me on my toes – you know, that can be a good thing – and one or two policemen to run away from. If you understand the sort of man I am and what I like, you'll know that it couldn't get much bigger and better than that. I was the man I wanted to be. Everything I had I wanted, and everything I wanted I had, except perhaps for a bit more money to pay off the HP, like most of us.

The next I knew, I opened my eyes and the sky was a blur and my head was a solid block of pain. I was on the ground. I'd fallen unconscious. I didn't know who or what had hit me, but I was badly hurt. Something was licking my face – it was my dog, Sandy, an Alsatian lurcher cross. He was whining. The licking didn't stop. I couldn't move. What had happened? I lost consciousness again. Some minutes later I came round, and I realized I was lying in the mud. I'd been out for I didn't know how long. There was no one else with me, except Sandy. My eyes were open. I could move now – my arms and legs weren't broken, and there was no tarmac or road around, so it couldn't have been a vehicle accident. But when I tried to sit up I felt sick and dizzy and veered close to losing consciousness again. It was my head – someone had knocked me down. I felt my face. One side was terribly swollen and blood poured from my nose. My cheekbone was smashed in. My jaw was all wrong; it hung down like someone had unhooked it. Whoever it was had hit me very hard – there wasn't any man who could do that with his fist, they'd used a bar or a hammer. Someone didn't just want to hurt me, they'd wanted to kill me.

I was in serious trouble.

I became more aware of my surroundings. The Mazda pick-up was right there, loaded with logs. The tractor was not far off, and the four-acre cover of oaks that we were meant to be clearing . . .

So I was at work. But where was Robin Dyer, the man I worked with? I remembered: today he'd had to go on a different job and I'd come up here on my own. I looked around. There was no house, no one else working here, not for miles. This copse was at the end of a long, rough track. I couldn't shout because of my dislocated jaw, but anyway no one would hear me. I was on my own with this.

There was only one way I was going to get out of there. I had to get into the pick-up and drive. I made it to the door of the cab and hauled myself in. I was in terrible pain. My co-ordination was shot to hell and I was near unconscious from one moment to the next. I saw my arms and legs working from a distance, as if they belonged to someone else. I had to drive without much sense of how far away things were because the eye on that right-hand side had closed up. Blood was pouring down my face and soaking into my shirt. My dislocated jaw made my breathing loud and rasping. I was frightened. I'd been in scrapes and accidents before, but this was of a different order. If I didn't get help I was going to die out here. I started up the Mazda and headed off, cross-country. Every jolt of the suspension caused bursts of pain in my jaw and skull.

The next I knew, I was slewed across any old how, in a layby, and I was coming round again from being unconscious. Obviously I'd felt myself giving out and had swung in here; now I was back again. Nothing had changed; it hadn't been a dream. The right-hand side of my face had ballooned. Blood ran down on to my shirt. Someone had given me a good hiding. I couldn't think who, or why. I put the truck in gear again and took off, slowly. I remember driving through Witheridge. My only thought was to get home.

The journey was a blur. Somehow I made it. I was back at Bishop's Nympton, standing in front of my own front door. I didn't know where the truck was. The door opened and Julie was there. I saw the shock hit her. The blood drained from her face; she went white as a sheet. She caught me as I stumbled forwards. I was on the verge of collapse.

Julie had the two little boys to think of, so it was Gordon Parker who drove me to the doctor. At Barnstaple hospital, once the swelling went down, they could really set to work. Dr Buchanan said I was like a vehicle in a crash-repair shop – and it took him a long time to fix me. He could see which direction the impact had come from and set about trying to push my cheekbone back out the same way it had been pushed in. The cheekbone had separated from the rest of my skull completely. If that blow had hit my nose, just a couple of inches to the left, it would have pushed into my brain and I'd have been killed. The operation involved cutting in a few inches back from my ear and then going in with tools, behind where the shattered sections of cheekbone now lay, so he could push them forward again.

Afterwards, I began to piece together what had happened. As it turned out, no one had hit me; it had been an accident. Tree-felling is dangerous work and you should always work in pairs. Robin Dyer had had to go on another job, but I'd carried on regardless. We were paid for the amount of ground we cleared. If I didn't get on and do it, there'd be nothing in my pocket for that day. It was on top of a hill, up an old farm track, and the work was to clear a small copse of oak – around four acres. The trees were substantial enough: two and a half to three feet through the middle. The work was the same as ever: cut down the stick, trim it down and cut the top off, then drag it – using the tractor – back to the loading bay, near the road, so the timber trucks with the hydraulic arms could get in and load them up at the end of the week.

I'd cut down an oak, trimmed the branches and cut off the top. OK so far. Then I'd jumped into the tractor and started reversing, ready to hook it up to the stick and haul it away. As I reversed, I looked over my right shoulder to see where I was going.

At the rear of the tractor was a big, heavy anchor, made of iron, which we put down when we needed to pull the trees over. When the tractor was moving, as it was now, the anchor was lifted by a hydraulic arm, hooked up to a heavy-duty chain, each link about as thick as a finger. One of the links in that chain broke. It had been corroded or there'd been a flaw in the weld.

Two things happened at once. Firstly, the heavy iron anchor dropped on to the ground with a thud and stalled the tractor – stopped it dead in its tracks. That turned out to be a godsend, because otherwise it would have kept on rolling backwards and I don't know where I'd have ended up. Secondly, at the same time, the hydraulic arm – a rod of heavy-gauge steel around four feet long and two inches thick – flew the other way, upwards, into the cab. It moved quicker than the eye could see and hit me on the cheekbone, just an inch below my eye, as I was looking over my shoulder. I was knocked un-conscious and thrown off the seat and down among the pedals. There was a hell of a lot of blood on that cab floor. I don't remember how I got out of there and back to my truck; the first I remember was Sandy licking my face to bring me round.

There were quite a few operations to put me right, and all the teeth in that side of my jaw went rotten and had to be taken out, nerves drilled out and all. Mr Cripps, the dentist in South Molton, performed wonders for me. I've only just finished my last treatment with him, thirty-five years later. There was a time when I had a plate at the top of my mouth, mounted with some of my false teeth. I was standing at a counter of a store, I think it was in South Molton, and there was some issue over a bill to be paid. So I was standing on my side of the counter talking about how much was this and how much was that. The rattly old plate flew out of my mouth and dropped on to the counter, two or three teeth sticking out of it. The man laughed and pointed at it and said, 'I don't want that. Just square up the bill, and that'll do.'

My teeth have been taken out, false ones put in, re-inforced, the works. The last bill I had only recently, decades later, was for £1,100. I dare say it won't end there.

Falling

"My strength was gone.
My pleasures I couldn't reach."

The accident knocked me for six. My nerve went. I fell far and hard. I lost my confidence, totally. I couldn't look at a chainsaw or a lumber yard. I was prescribed Valium. I went from a man at the top of his game, having just bought his own home, to being off work on twenty-one weeks' statutory sick pay of £29.90 per week. It was more than depression, it was shock that had run through my system like a bolt of lightning and made me afraid of life itself. I was having a nervous breakdown. There was no picking myself up and dusting myself down, like after other accidents I'd had. However much I wanted to, this time I found it wasn't possible. That nerve had snapped as surely as the chain itself; it wouldn't do the work, wouldn't lift me. I was wretched, I truly was down. I couldn't even go into a pub. I sat at home, my head in my hands.

As time went on, it didn't get better, it got worse. Things I would ordinarily have coped with put me further down. I went to a darts meeting one Sunday night, a regular thing at the Tiverton Inn. I'd been captain of the darts team there, and it was run by my wife's Uncle Dick and Auntie Marion, both of whom I was very fond of. No sooner had I got up the courage to go in than I found Marion, who ran the bar, in a state of shock. She latched on to me straight away. 'Johnny, I don't know what to do,' she said in a low voice so that others couldn't hear. 'Can you go to the kitchen, because I think Dick might be … dead.' While she carried on serving I walked on out the back. Dick was sitting in a chair in there, his chin lowered on to his chest. He had that white look, that stillness, which only comes with death. I didn't need to check his pulse; I knew he was. I walked straight back into the bar and told Marion, 'Yes, he's dead.' I knocked back a whisky as if it were a drop of water. I was a gravedigger; I was used to death. I'd had a lot to do with dead bodies over the years, I'd been scared in graveyards, and by the power of nature itself.

I remembered back to the time when I'd gone to stay with my sister and the most terrible storm broke out directly overhead. The thunder was deafening and the lightning showed up the whole sky. My little boy Stuart and I were sharing a room. The window was open. Outside was the graveyard, so these flashes of light made the gravestones suddenly come very close, very bright. Stuart had been frightened, and so was I. In the window stood a decoration, one of those metal cut-outs, and I remember it was in the shape of an owl. The lightning made it come alive; you'd almost expect it to fly across the room. We didn't know if we could sleep. The next thing was, there was this tremendous burst of light and a crack of thunder and that owl *did* fly across the room. It had been struck by lightning. It left that windowsill and hit the opposite wall. I shouted and swore and Derek and Shirley came rushing in, Shirley in her pink nightie. Stuart was crying his heart out. We worked out what had happened and shut the window, and battened down the hatches to try and get through the night without mishap. That had been fear, all right – the sense of danger, of a great power much bigger than me that made me feel like the smallest, most unimportant speck . . .

And this fear now was almost the same – like panic. There was no way of looking up. It was a crushing weight on my shoulders.

I would stay and help Marion, of course I would. I waited for the undertakers, and during that wait all the sadness in the world seemed to crowd into that kitchen. There was a dark cloud over us. It got me in a bad way. When the undertakers arrived Ray Setherton and I helped lift Uncle Dick into what we call the shell coffin – the one they used to transport bodies back to the chapel of rest. At the undertakers' we undressed him. The lady there washed the body, as usual, and we dressed him again so he was fit for burial. How near we all were to death – and how close I was to it again, now, lifting this man whom I'd known so well into his coffin. He'd gone. He was just so much hundredweight. It made me feel so bad. If my nerve was broke before, now I couldn't even find the ends to try and mend it.

My wife looked at me, my children looked at me, and my despair was mirrored in their eyes. Their disappointment killed me. My strength was gone. My pleasures I couldn't reach. I was earning no money. My family was going downhill. I looked a mess, with my broken face.

Dr Gleddle was worried. The Valium he'd prescribed to try and help with the depression wasn't working, and there was a danger I'd become dependent on the drug. The doctor said, 'Johnny, I want you to go and see someone.'

'What d'you mean, like a vicar?'

'That's odd, why d'you say that?'

'Don't know, just came into my head.'

'Well, as it happens, yes, this man is a vicar. I'm not sending you to him to have you believe in God, but he's a man who's good at dealing with people who are in trouble the way you are.'

'All right. I'll go and see him.'

'He's called Reverend Pennington.'

I was given a date and a time, and the name of a house in North Molton, a neighbouring village. It turned out to be a terraced cottage right in front of the church. Another church. These old buildings have been so important in my life, right from when I attended choir with Mother, to the digging of graves in their shadow – and now, as I approached this house, sure enough there it was, a church, watching over what would happen.

When I rang the bell up at Revd Pennington's house I didn't know what to expect. The door was opened by a tall man, perhaps in his sixties, baldish, wearing glasses. He had the look of a gentleman type. He'd been born in Hartland in North Devon, I believe, but had lived for many years in North Molton. He said in this very slow, careful voice, 'Ahhh . . . yessss . . . Come in . . .' I stubbed out a cigarette before stepping over the threshold. 'Now, tell me,' he said in the same careful way, 'how . . . many of those do you smoke . . . every day?'

'Around forty,' I replied. 'Player's Weights.'

'Hmm, well . . . It might be a good thing . . . to cut down the number . . . a bit.'

Revd Pennington showed me into the front room of his house. It had old-fashioned furniture, as you can imagine, all beautifully looked after and spotlessly clean. A chair stood in the corner with a standard lamp beside it, and the curtains were closed. There was a calm and peaceful atmosphere and I immediately felt that this was a man who was kind and interested in people, and that he understood what it was like to be low in spirits. At the same time he had a natural authority; you could feel that from his voice, how he spoke. He looked at me and almost the first thing he said was, 'Now tell me, do you ever go to sleep?'

'Well, yes. Every night.'

'I see,' he said. 'Would you sit in that chair in the corner and show me how?'

'How what?'

'Show me how you might go to sleep. Just so I can see for myself.'

I went and sat in the chair he'd indicated. The standard lamp was there, to one side of the chair, so what with the light falling on the chair as well it was a bit like I was on a stage, doing this performance for him. I leaned back in the chair and made like I was in a position to go to sleep. 'Put your left hand on your left knee,' he instructed me. I did so. 'Now see if you can lift up that same hand,' he went on.

I tried – but I couldn't. My own hand refused to move. It lay there as if it belonged to someone else. I kept trying – but no, I couldn't lift it up. That scared me. He looked me straight in the eye and said very calmly, 'One, two, three – and there, now you can move it all right, can't you?'

Sure enough, I could. This was hypnosis, I knew that, of course, but it was a very odd sensation, even if you did know in theory what was happening.

The next I knew, he put his hand on my head and I felt the gentleness of that touch. There was something in

his manner and in the way he laid on hands 'that broke through all resistance and went straight to the heart.

He said no more than a few words and I was under.

When I awoke, it wasn't like coming round from a normal sleep. I felt woozy, as if I'd been drugged, or on a long journey. Revd Pennington said, 'You . . . haven't slept . . . for a very long time.'

'How d'you mean?' I asked. I was a bit surprised. I slept every night, same as everyone else.

'I've taken you back to the age of six years old,' he said, 'and I can tell you . . . that you haven't slept . . . not properly, mind, not like you should sleep . . . not in all that time.'

The truth dawned. It was because of my sleep-walking. I told him, then, about my father having to tie the windows shut upstairs, with all my re-enacting the day's events in my sleep. He listened, nodded. 'There you are. That's what I mean. It's going to be important for you to learn to sleep properly. The only reason that sleep exists . . . is to give the mind . . . a place . . . and the time . . . to be refreshed. To mend itself. And this is what your mind needs to do . . . now.'

When I left the house, I felt deeply affected by what had happened and by the special qualities of Revd Pennington. It really had turned my mind upside down. I was dying for a fag. I got in the car and lit up.

That cigarette tasted like poison. It was enough to make you sick. I coughed and spat, I wrenched open the car door and threw the cigarette down on the ground and got out and stamped on it.

The next morning I tried again to smoke a cigarette and it was the same – it tasted poisonous.

I went back twice to Revd Pennington's house. He didn't hypnotize me again. He would just say in that very slow voice, 'Ah . . . Johnny . . . How are you?' and then we'd sit together and he'd listen, and I'd tell him everything. There was a quality to his listening that made you feel that every word you said was valuable, and that in telling him, the worries and troubles and sadness were taken away, and one by one vanished into thin air.

I haven't smoked a cigarette since the first time I left his house. I had seven Player's Weights left in the packet and I put them on the windowsill and looked at them every morning. They were there for years. We had to clean the cobwebs off and dust underneath them, but they stayed there. I kept them on purpose to remind me that I didn't smoke. They must have gone stale as hell but one day, years later, I went to have a look – and there were only six left. A day or two later there were five. And so on. Someone was taking these dried-up stale old things and smoking them. It was Craig – he must have been fourteen or fifteen at that time. It made me smile. Sure enough, like any kid, he wanted to try the fags.

I had another reason to be glad to know Revd Pennington. Some years later, Julie was diagnosed with breast cancer. I phoned to tell him, and when he heard what I had to say, he repeated the same words three times over. It was as if he was controlling what happened, in the words, in the way he delivered them over the phone. His faith would bend circumstances the way he wanted – he was sure of that. 'She . . . will be . . . cured,' he said, quietly and certainly.

And again, 'She will be cured.'

'She will . . . be . . . cured.'

I'd been frightened sick at the hospital. I went straight from there to the Black Cock and downed several whiskies in a row. The landlady, Sandra, asked, 'What's the matter?'

'It's Julie,' I replied. 'She's got breast cancer.'

Sandra replied, 'You know, that's odd. A man came in this pub only yesterday – I never saw him before, and he left a sealed envelope and asked me to give it to the first person who came in who needed help.' She went to fetch this envelope; it was tucked in amongst the optics. 'You'd better take it, then,' she said.

When I got home I opened it. Inside was a card with a picture of a beautiful shoreline. On the reverse of the card was printed, *'Please read this card very carefully and put it on your mantelpiece . . .'* It was a healing card, which claimed it would heal the person who held it in their possession.

Some time later I drove Julie to the hospital for her operation. She had seen the card, and hadn't torn it up and thrown it away. She'd kept it on the mantelpiece. Now we were in the car, ready to meet our fate. When we were passing through Landkey, she suddenly asked me, 'D'you think this lump has changed?' I dared not hope, but an expression of Mother's sprang to mind: 'If it's movable, it's curable.' I thought about the stranger walking into the pub and leaving that card, and how Julie had read it, and how we'd kept it on the mantelpiece. And above all I remembered the strange, certain way that Revd Pennington had told me down the phone, 'She will be cured,' three times over.

There was a whole lot of people's good will, or willpower you might say, all concentrating on this illness, not least that of the doctors and surgeons and nurses who helped us so much at the hospital.

When they operated on Julie, the lump was found to be non-malignant. It did seem like a miracle, how completely the threat was lifted from her life.

If it wasn't for Revd Pennington, I don't think I'd be here today. He's well over ninety years old now. He was such a fine vicar and helped many people without ever thinking of charging them. I'd like to know how many others he hypnotized in order to help them give up

smoking, but the sad part is that his beloved wife smoked heavily, and of course in the way of these things he never could persuade her to give up. But she lived to a good age, anyway. After she passed away Revd Pennington moved down to South Devon so that he could be near his daughter. And the writing of this book is an opportunity for me and my wife and children to send him this message: God be with you and your family, and thank you for everything you've done for us.

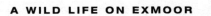

PART THREE

A new start

" . . . all the wonder and beauty of nature
is apparent in the goings-on of any
common creature. **"**

was no longer a lost soul, but I was still in trouble. I had no money. Somehow I had to climb out of this hole I was in. Many friends helped me through this bad time, and they were to prove my salvation.

Mike Warren, best mate for forty-three years, helped me a great deal in the aftermath of the accident. He drove me out to where it happened and we pieced together the chain of events – exactly what had happened and why. We had to gather evidence for insurance purposes. It was Mike who went and found the tractor, so we could examine it and determine that the chain had broken. Mike has been a brilliant friend to me in countless ways over the years and has always been so kind to our family. He has the nickname Spider, although I don't use it, I call him Brother. He recently retired, and we had a great weekend celebrating.

Robin Dyer, my partner at work at the time of the accident, is very ill at the time of writing, in a home in Taunton. He's not able to speak, but he can laugh, and he did laugh when he last saw me. It's difficult to see a fit, strong man brought low like this. You begin to wonder where your God is, when you see that. I pray for him – as he did for me when I was down.

The other person who helped me at that time, as it turned out, unwittingly opened the door to a new life for me. It is a small thing he did, among countless other small kindnesses people showed me that won't get a mention, but this one gesture changed everything, and, although I'd never have guessed it at the time, it shaped the way I was to live my life and the kind of man I was to become.

He lent me his video camera.

The man's name is Roger Gregory. The Gregory clan is a famous one hereabouts, they're a big family of entrepreneurs with all sorts of successful businesses, from egg-packing to transport. Roger runs a contract-cleaning business now. He has been a good friend of mine for God knows how long.

These days, of course, everyone and his wife has a video camera – or camcorder – and most of them fit in the palm of your hand and offer digital quality on a big screen. At that time, though, a video camera was an unusual piece of equipment. This is going back before Super VHS, before VHS, before Hi-8, to what they called 8mm videotape. Your actual magnetic tape turned round on spools inside the machine, which will seem pretty old-fashioned to young people now. It would have cost quite a lot of money and it wasn't nothing to lend it out – but he told me, yes, go on take it, without a second thought.

I'd always been good at art at school, and I'd taken photographs on an old Brownie box camera when I was a child. I still have a few of them. There is a picture of a horse, and one of a cow, and one of a sheep.

So I went down to Park House in South Molton, where Roger lived, and picked up the camera, and then drove up to Molland Moor. At Ridgeway Cross I turned right and went through Molland Moor Gate on to Anstey Common. I parked up by the landmark known as Hancock Stone. I was right on top of Exmoor now. This was the ground I knew and loved so well. Many people visit Exmoor; they come for the landscape, the ponies, the red deer. It's a wilderness, in a way, but one of such beauty that you'd think it had been lansdscaped by the most famous artist you can imagine. A series of huge, open moorland hills, quite gentle in contour and shape, are intersected by steep-sided wooded valleys. The open hills make you feel like you're walking on clouds planted with bell heather and gorse, while the valleys give Exmoor its secrecy, and provide cover and shelter for its wildlife. Through these valleys tumble clear streams, sometimes racing over boulders and through rough heath and woodland, other times meandering along flat-bottomed flood plains.

Anyway, there I was, up on Exmoor. I took out my

field glasses and I could see a herd of deer just where I thought they might be – maybe a mile away as the crow flies, on the top of the next hill. Between us was a valley. I would see how close I could get to them, and then I would film them.

I attended to the camera – I wanted to make sure it was switched to standby so that I was ready for anything to happen. Then I set off. The slope down to the river was very steep, maybe a 75 per cent gradient, the heather dotted with large boulders. Every now and again I checked the wind direction. I hit the bottom of the valley and went through the river, carrying the camera high to avoid splashing it. These were the skills I'd used for stalking, all those years, except that now, instead of carrying a rifle, it was a different implement I was holding up above my head – a camera.

With my boots and trousers soaking wet, I climbed up the other side, through a dense cover of gorse. When I was nearly at the top I pulled down my face mask, so that I was camouflaged from top to bottom with just eye holes and a gauze to breathe through. I came to the edge of the grassland and dropped to a slow crawl, pushing the camera ahead of me. I moved very slowly and quietly. I came to the fence that divided the top land from the valley and rested the lens of the camera on the bottom wire. I looked through the viewfinder. Just twenty yards away was a large group of hinds and yearlings. They were so close. My heart was thumping; the adrenalin raced around my system.

I tagged the little red button on the camera to set the tape going – that was my trigger, now. I filmed them for maybe fifteen minutes.

My eye has been trained since earliest childhood to seek out and notice wildlife, and carrying this camera sharpened the senses in the same way that carrying a rifle, or a wire, or a gaffe, or a pellet of ammunition had done. But, having been so badly hurt myself, I found it was no longer so easy to hurt or kill a living creature. This was like hunting, but it was also something else. It was capturing wildlife, but it was letting them go at the same time. There was the thrill of the chase and I could take home what I'd caught, but the creatures themselves were left undisturbed.

When I'd finished filming I wriggled backwards, dead slow, quiet. Having reached the cover of the gorse and trees, I stood up and scrambled down to the river and up the other side of the valley. I traipsed back over the plateau to where I'd parked.

When I arrived at the vehicle I paused for a moment and took out the field glasses to find the deer again. There they were. And they hadn't moved, not one bit. I'd come and gone without them knowing.

I drove home, thinking of what had just happened, of the feeling that had come over me. When I was walking up on the moor carrying that Sony camera, something in me had come back to life. After my accident I'd fallen into such low spirits as I'd never imagined, and instead of looking outwards, to what was happening around me, I'd only been able to look inwards, at my own hurt and loss of confidence. I'd fallen, and Revd Pennington had stopped my fall. But when I'd carried that camera out on the moor, I'd started to look up again at what was around, what was happening in nature. And I'd wanted to shoot it – with the camera. Now I wanted to take home my prey not in the back of the van, bloodied and ready for the butcher, but on videotape, so that it might be seen over and over, and give pleasure to myself and others. Suddenly, I felt excited to be alive.

I got back home to Bishop's Nympton and hurried indoors. I put the camera up on the table, plugged it in and switched it to playback. I squared up to the TV and thumbed the button. The tape rolled.

First of all there was a long section of heather and grass and a few boulders, very close up, swinging wildly in the frame. Then there was a brief glimpse of river – blurred silvery water rushing over stones. Thirdly there was a whole lot of gorse and the sound of me, panting away. Then the fence came into view, and slowly, inch by inch, it came closer. At this point the picture went blank. It stopped dead. No deer, nothing.

Just when I'd thought I was switching the camera on, I had turned it off. Disaster.

It was disappointing after all that effort. Of course I felt stupid. I should return the camera to Roger Gregory and forget all about it.

There was a serious lack of money, for my family, after the accident. We were on sickness benefit for many months. After a while, when my face had mended enough, I could go back to digging graves occasionally, like before. But the first full-time job I had was as a farm labourer up at Sindercombe, an Exmoor farm owned by Herbert Thorne. He was a short, stocky man with a blustery, round red face. He had sandy hair and wore it sideways, kept there with a lick of Brylcreem, and he had a thick Devon accent. He lived on his own in the farmhouse, his wife having died some years earlier. He was exceptionally kind to me – and he was the best type of farmer you could hope for. He loved his two or three hundred sheep and he loved his fat bullocks. It was my job to feed them their cake, and they never went short. These were the days, mind, when you could take a sheep to market and get £60 for it. That was a serious amount of money.

Raymond Coles also worked with me on Mr Thorne's farm. He was a big strong man; he's a driving instructor now. He, too, was very fond of Herbert. He said something to me once that would later come to mind. He'd noticed that Herbert would get easily worked up over his dog. Like most collies, it was devoted to its master, never mind that Herbert shouted at it from time to time. Herbert didn't smoke and had only the occasional beer, but he must have had high blood pressure because he went very red in the face if that dog went the wrong way or did the wrong thing. Raymond Coles said to me, 'He's going to have a heart attack if he doesn't watch out.'

We were happy, working at Sindercombe. Everything had to be 100 per cent, from the hedging and making up the banks, the repair of the buildings and the equipment, to the condition of the stock – and that made us proud. I can remember walking the cows three miles up to the top of the moor to find new grazing. In fact, this taking up of the stock on to the high ground for summer grazing is an ancient tradition on Exmoor, which used to be that much of a sheep factory, in the old days, that there were four specially designed places for counting sheep positioned around the moor, and farmers had their sheep counted up on the moor at the beginning of summer and counted back down again at the end.

I grew so fond of Herbert, it was without even thinking about it that I'd go up there in the middle of the night, if necessary, to help him start up the old Lister diesel engine that pumped his water out of the valley. He became like part of our family. He had a sister too, who helped him. She had a withered hand on the end of a short arm, but still managed to ride a horse out.

Raymond Coles, the man I worked with, knew me pretty well by reputation and when I told him about an idea I had of buying my own video camera and photographing wildlife, he told me – friendly like – that he didn't think I'd have the patience to do that kind of thing. But that was the one thing I'd already developed over a lifetime of stalking and keeping animals. I had all the patience in the world because, for me, waiting had always been the way I'd got what I wanted.

And perhaps he didn't quite understand how much I loved wildlife, and always had done since I was a boy. I was building up a small farm in my back garden in Bishop's Nympton. I took in all sorts of animals. It was the done thing in those days to drown kittens, but when Herbert's cat had a litter of five, I asked if I could save one, take it home to keep. She was black with four white socks and we called her Smoky. She lived in our house for eighteen years – we loved that cat. She had a stroke eventually, started walking sideways. We called the vet and he said, 'Ah, it's Smoky, I'd better come out.' He knew, you see, that Smoky refused to go to the vet. Oh, no. We once tried to put her in a cat basket and she ripped out three of her own claws on the plastic mesh, she was that frantic. So the vet knew he had to come out. This time there was nothing he could do and by half past six Smoky was put down.

It wasn't just the kitten I took home from

Sindercombe. There were four lambs that I was having to bottle-feed. Every year during lambing you have one or two that slip through the net and end up being bottle-fed for one reason or another. Perhaps the mother rejects them, or she'd died. Or maybe she doesn't have the milk to feed twins and the weakest begins to melt away, and so you have to take over with the bottle. If a lamb is stillborn, you can skin it and make a coat for a live lamb to wear so that the dead one's mother will accept it and give it milk, but the timing has to be right for that to happen. And of course bottle-fed lambs become very tame. Four of them joined the little farm in our back garden. I made up a little enclosure there. The lambs and the dogs played together on my front lawn, especially the black ram, called Blackie, and Sandy, my lurcher cross. They gambolled around like they were brother and sister. Sandy loved that ram.

I also had a bantam in the back garden, which sat on eight Aylesbury duck eggs and hatched them all. You can imagine how far such a little bird had to stretch herself to cover eight Aylesbury eggs – they're as big as a buzzard's. They all hatched out fine. This little bantam would cross the lawn, proud as anything of the huge Aylesbury ducklings waddling after her. For ducks, it's so important they have water to wash themselves in, so I filled up a big dustbin and put it out there – except that when they dried their feathers, shaking them out, muddy water went all over next door's white sheets hanging on the washing line. She was good as gold about it.

I brought back chickens from Sindercombe as well. I ended up with so many roosters it was havoc, what with their fighting and crowing all day. I had to kill them – fourteen, there were – and I put them in the freezer. I thought we'd eat them, though in the event I couldn't bring myself to do it. These fourteen frozen carcasses kept on rising to the top of the freezer, and I'd put them down the bottom, and up they'd pop again, and so it went on. A year or two passed with the frozen roosters going up and down. Then I asked my neighbours on the other side, Mary and Frank Crook, 'Here, d'you like chicken?'

'Yes,' they said, and they ate all fourteen. One by one, mind, not all at once.

I've been lucky with my neighbours and because they know how much I love animals I'm always called on when there's a creature in trouble – frogs and moles and all sorts.

So Raymond Coles, when I first started working with him, had only heard about the sort of wild man I was – the fighting and the drinking and the rifle-shooting and the snares, the trout-tickling, the explosions in the river, the car crashes and the pub fights – and with the best will in the world that didn't fit with his idea of a wildlife cameraman. It was even true to say that once while I was at work two men in uniform turned up to arrest me right in front of Raymond's eyes, but it turned out to be Brian Leatherby, my friend from the army in Hong Kong, who, along with his partner, was now a champion trainer of police dogs. He'd come to look me out, and fooled all of us.

Raymond changed his mind about me, though, when he saw me with my own video camera, waiting dead still in the same spot, up against the hedge, for a full hour. I wanted to capture the antics of a blue tit perched on a bramble there. It was the sort of thing that most people pass by without noticing. The blue tit is not a rare bird; they're all over the place. But if you wait, and go closer and watch for longer, then all the wonder and beauty of nature is apparent in the goings-on of any common creature. It's enough to take your breath away. Raymond walked past and I was still there, staring at that bramble, waiting.

One morning I turned up for work and Herbert wasn't around, so I went about my business as usual. As I walked past the house I saw that his curtains were still drawn, which was odd. I loaded up the link box with bales of hay to take down to the Cheviot ewes. It was 29 January and biting cold, the coldest on record; they'd need extra rations. My breath was a thick cloud in front of my face, and I had all the gloves and hats and coats I needed. I drove on past the big shed. Beyond that, on the left, there was a cover of blackthorn trees and I caught a glimpse of a big stag lying in there – just a twitch of movement. I stamped on the brake and stopped the tractor to have a look. As I watched, part of the picture came away and I saw it was a dog moving off. It was Herbert's dog, the one he shouted at from time to time. And that brown colour wasn't a stag at all, it was a man's coat. What I was looking at, in fact, was Herbert Thorne's hand sticking up in the air.

I got off the tractor and ran over. He was lying dead, of a heart attack. The dog had stayed with him all through that bitterly cold night, faithful to the end. It was a terrible sight. You could see that the life had been swept from him in one big *whoosh* of pain and shock. I was terribly upset. Herbert had become like one of my own family; he was a kind and good man. He didn't deserve to die all alone in the freezing cold. He'd obviously gone out to check his sheep last thing at night and hadn't made it back. Those words of Raymond's came to me: 'He's going to have a heart attack . . .'

We called the police, and when they came up to the site of Herbert's death they tried to bundle him into the back of a short-wheel-base Land Rover like he was a piece of rubbish. I grew very upset. 'No. This is not right,' I said, and physically stopped them. 'This man deserves better.' I walked back to the farm and called Mike Disborough, from the Black Cock, who came straight out, and together we fashioned a makeshift stretcher out of a section of wooden hayrick. We went out and lifted Herbert on to it and carried him with dignity back to the house. We laid him on the settee, and waited with him until the undertakers arrived.

I dug Herbert's grave, at Twitchen. His wife had died some years before, and I opened up her grave so that he could join her. It was a big funeral, as was fitting for a man so well liked. It was one of those times when I went to the funeral as well as dug the grave. I found a spot to change my clothes and went into the church to join in prayers for his good soul. If anyone deserved a heaven, it was Herbert Thorne.

The gravedigging was regular work and I was often to be found in a graveyard at 4.30 to 5 in the morning, digging away peacefully, before the sun was up. It was hot work and the heat would make it twice as hard. However, to be standing in a grave, in a half-dark churchyard, all on your own, is scary. You learn not to give rein to your imagination.

Nearly all the lads in the village have had a go at helping me dig graves at one time or another. One week I had eight of them to do – you need help to get through that. These lads and I came across all sorts of bones and skulls and wedding rings, and so on. It can be said I've often stolen game and salmon from people who might lay claim to owning it, but I'd never dream of taking a grain of gold out of a grave.

And there was additional work. Apart from digging the graves, you had to make everything right for when the mourners turned up – check for mice and frogs that might have got into the hole you've dug. When the coffin is being lowered they don't want a distraction like that, a little creature hopping about in the bottom there. The grave has to be lined with green matting to make it look a touch less like a hole in the ground. And the green matting makes a more acceptable surface for the mourners to stand on, plus the spoil is often covered. It soothes people if their loved one's remains are looked after in a civilized way. And of course it's important that these preparations are completed on time, before the mourners come out from the service. It's not good to be seen at your work. I was standing in a grave I'd dug, once, when I saw a lady dressed all in black coming up the road. She was late; the service was already under way in the church, and the path would bring her right alongside the grave. I didn't think I should be seen. I ducked down and waited for her to pass. I could hear her footsteps and I crouched lower. Then, just when the footsteps were loudest, they slowed down and stopped altogether. She'd taken one step sideways, to look into the grave. I popped up – curly-headed, naked torso covered in tattoos – and I must have looked like an escaped convict. She leaped four or five inches off the ground, she was so startled. I immediately had both hands in the air, saying over and over, 'I'm so sorry, I'm just getting the grave ready . . .' It was her turn to make me feel better. 'That's quite all right,' she said and we smiled at each other, and she carried on into the church.

Some graveyards were more difficult than others. At Filleigh we had a serious problem with groundwater. I was working for Steve Westacott once and even while we dug the grave we had a pump working full time to take out the water. We kept it going all during the service, and we stationed Jane Westacott by the corner of the church as a lookout. She appeared and waved at us when the coffin and the mourners were coming. We looked sharp and pulled out the pump. I poured a load of sawdust in the bottom, which I hoped would help soak up the water so that the coffin didn't make a splash. As the mourners approached, water was already filling the bottom of the grave and floating this layer of sawdust upwards. The vicar said his words pretty quickly, but even more water flooded in. He knew about our problem, so he'd walked briskly and he'd shortened his speech. He'd tried his hardest, and it was all a bit of a rush. At last we could lower the coffin. It went down with a *plop*! as it hit the water. It floated, bobbing about down there. As the relatives threw in their handfuls of earth the coffin was slowly rising, all the time. It was all I could do not to shout at them to come on and hurry up.

When the mourners had gone we jumped in and stood on the coffin. It was like being on the deck of a boat – tipping this way and that. We jumped up and down and our weight began to push it under the water. We had to hurry and throw down big clats of earth on top for weight, so we could get out. We managed to put that coffin in the earth, but it was a close thing. For a moment I thought it was going to float to the top and sail down the path. Six months later I had to go back and put more earth in. In fact, if I ever had to open up a grave in Filleigh churchyard, the coffins were always intact – the rot is so much less if there's complete saturation.

I shall never forget the time I had to reopen a tomb in South Molton. Not a grave, mind, but a tomb, a family vault. It was a massive great thing, with four names on it from this particular family. There was one slot left under there, for the lady who had just died. She was 103 years old. That is a long, long life. Our task was to open this vault and put her in alongside her relatives. There were four inches of turf on top of this massive block of solid concrete, the lid of the tomb, so I had to hire a compressor and a hammer drill to cut a two-foot-square opening through six-inch-thick concrete. As the debris fell in you could hear a splash as it hit the water at the bottom – and there was quite a delay, so it was a deep hole. Eventually we could poke a ladder in and I pulled on wellies and squeezed down through the opening. I had a torch with me and the beam pointed every which way as I descended, step by step. It was freezing cold and there was this awful smell – difficult to describe, but it was a kind of bitterness, which left a metallic taste on your tongue. Down and down I went, colder and colder. It made the hairs stand up on the back of my neck, knowing there were four bodies in here somewhere.

When I reached the bottom I stepped off the ladder into 10 inches of water. I pointed the torch, looked for the bodies. Where were they? I put the beam of light down through the water underfoot. Nothing. I shouted up, 'There's no one here!'

'Where's 'un to, then?' came the call from above. 'Muss be somewhere. D'you see 'em on the way down?'

'No, nothin' here, no one.'

I stepped on to the ladder again and began to climb. As I approached the top, suddenly they were right next to me, all four of them, laid on shelves cut into the sides of the tomb, one on top of the other. And because the wood of the coffins had rotted to nothing the torchlight picked up every detail of hair and bones, and the clothing rotting away to pieces on those bones, and the fingernails and the teeth and the eye sockets . . . It frightened the daylights out of me. I almost fell off the ladder. 'Christ! Found 'em!' I tried to shout, but it took a couple of goes for my voice to work properly.

'Is there room for 'er?' came the call from the square of daylight above me. I pointed the torch, but for the life of me I couldn't see where we might fit our new resident. It was full up. We couldn't just turf someone off their

shelf. Then I noticed that there was one more ledge, but it was right in under the concrete lip of the tomb. It was going to be the devil of a job to get her down through that opening and then up on to that ledge. None the less, that's what we'd have to do.

It was a small service, as you might expect from someone so very old. Most of those who'd known her had long gone. Prayers were said and handfuls of earth thrown on the coffin as it lay in the open air. When everyone had gone we set to work – and it was comical. I went down the ladder and then she had to be pitched upright, so she went down through the hole feet first. I had to take the full weight of her and the coffin and then climb down the ladder, without falling off, and without dropping her. Then I had this difficult manoeuvre, to twist her feet round and lift her up on to the ledge. There was only an inch or two of clearance. It was a hell of a job. I was sweating and swearing and straining. I hope she forgave me the indignity. I hope she was laughing at us. Eventually, though, we got her into place, tight as a drum, and there she still lies, reunited with her relatives from long ago.

A different type of shooting

". . . each time one of them returned I pressed the button on the remote and put another few inches of tape through the camera. **"**

The first camera I bought was a Sony Handicam 8mm, and I learned to use it in the back garden one spring, as the birds started nesting. I knew not to go too close and to wait until the chicks were half grown. By this time the parent birds would be to and fro more often, having to work harder, and there'd be no danger of my spoiling things, because a parent bird will abandon eggs or very young chicks if they think it's not safe – and a big hairy tattooed man poking his camera into their nests can be frightening. Birds are nervous creatures at the same time as being fierce protectors of their young.

Once I understood how the camera worked, I went further afield. Still not very far, mind, just into the village. Or I'd take the camera with me when I went gravedigging. I took lots of shots in the local church-yards. The song thrush was a favourite, but there aren't so many; they're a lucky find. Blackbirds were plentiful and a great bird to film. They love nesting in the ivy climbing up the graveyard walls. So I'd be digging and at the same time keeping an eye, as I always did, on what the wildlife was up to. Then I'd pick up my camera and work out how to get close enough.

Just like with hunting of any kind, getting close to any wild animal requires camouflage, silence, stillness, and making sure no scent reaches them. These were the skills I'd developed over a lifetime; they were second nature to me.

I changed camera again, to a Panasonic using VHS videotape, so that I could take the cassette out of the camera and put it straight into the player at home. I bought a double player, from Super VHS to ordinary VHS, which meant that just by pressing the pause button on the second machine I could make rough edits to the pictures, and cut out the rubbish. Hire purchase also allowed me to buy another important piece of equipment: a remote-control lead which plugged into the side of the camera, 100 feet long. The first time I used this was on a long-tailed tit's nest. The cock bird is a pinky colour with a very long tail and this pair had built a nest close to the Black Cock Inn, in a gorse bush in the lane there. Bob Cockram had noticed them at work and showed me where the nest was. I pushed the camera tripod in under the gorse bush, fixed the camera on top and plugged in the remote-control lead. Then I stuck a load of sprigs of gorse and leaves to the whole assembly to disguise it, and backed off down the lane maybe 70 feet, taking the lead with me. There I waited, on the corner, pretty much out of sight but able to see what was going on through field glasses.

Both male and female long-tailed tits were building the nest, and each time one of them returned I pressed the button on the remote and put another few inches of tape through the camera. They'd already made the outside of the nest – a mixture of moss and lichen – in an oblong shape, like a marrow stood on its end, with a hole on top. It's a very neat job they do, tidy as a chaffinch's. Now, as I filmed, they were carrying feathers to make the warm lining. Someone once counted the number of feathers long-tailed tits gathered for one nest – 280, collected and brought back and put into position. That is a lot of work for two little birds and it's just the lining. It was wonderful to film. For me, that was breath-taking excitement, with my camera up so close, only inches away from the action.

I came back three weeks later and saw them taking out droppings, which told me that their young had been born. I filmed again, and caught the tips of the babies' beaks poking out the hole at the top of the nest. When the parent appeared, he'd dip right down inside, disappearing completely except for that very long tail.

The next time I visited the nest, it was on the floor, broken. I like to think the young had flown, but I can't be sure. There are many predators who might have destroyed it – magpies, jackdaws, or one of us. But I felt in my bones they'd been lucky, and flown.

When I got the pictures home, I was over the moon. Up there on the screen was all the work of the long-tailed tit, in detail. I felt so excited to have done this. I kept my finger on the pause button to leave out the boring bits, and in the end I cut together a film – using this and other material I'd gathered – which lasted one and a half hours. I'd learned by now to talk as I was filming, so the narration was spontaneous. It was best like that. I was so pleased with my film that I decided to book the village hall in Bishop's Nympton, and put up a notice on the church wall to say that anyone who wanted could come along at that time, on that date, and see it. I charged a small entrance fee and I hoped that I might even sell a few copies of the film afterwards.

Come the day, I went along to the village hall and set up a 22-inch colour television and arranged the school-type chairs around it.

I was nervous. I knew I had enough friends and family coming for the hall not to be empty, but would the general public turn out? I just didn't know.

Yes, was the answer. They did. They took their seats, and there I was, standing up in front of fifty or sixty people, with my little television and the player and my home-made film. I welcomed everyone and without further ado showed them the film. Afterwards I talked about what I'd done. This went on for a long time, because people had so many questions, and the answers raised more questions. It gave me such immense satisfaction to talk to people about what I'd seen and done. I realized then, as I came away from that village hall – me and Julie loading up the telly and the player in the pick-up and stacking the chairs back how we'd found them – what a great love of wildlife there is in our country, in villages like this up and down the land. I saw how much we sympathize with the smallest, humblest creatures, and how much pleasure we get from learning about – and seeing up close – their habits, and their way of surviving and breeding, and the terrors they face from predators. Whether we live in the countryside or in the town, we love our animals.

Now, as I went around the village and the surrounding area, as I dug graves in the churchyards, as I carried my tripod and camera here and there, picking up shots, people would stop and ask me if I was going to make another film. Yes, I'd reply, some time soon. Watch this space.

I changed my camera to a Canon Hi8. Video technology was developing very fast, and I wanted the best-quality pictures I could get.

Someone asked me to film their wedding. I did it, and after that came more weddings, and kids' football matches. It was a way of making a living and practising with the camera. At North Molton they built a little tower next to the pitch so that I could stand up there on this platform, umbrella over my head to keep the rain off, and tape the match from a good vantage point. Football matches were OK, but weddings were stressful – it was so important to get it right. You had to get your shots, but without mucking up the service itself. At Bishop's Nympton, Revd Tull used to tick me off for moving around the church too much. He was well liked, but strict. When I think back to weddings, I just remember running about, up and down the path, in and out the church, round and round the graveyard, trying to get all the important shots – the ring on the finger, the walk down the aisle, the arrival, the departures, and so on. It was frantic and energetic work. At Pilton church in Barnstaple, I was outside once, walking back-wards, filming away, when the back of my heel came up against something and I pitched backwards and lay sprawled on someone's grave.

I'd often be asked to tape the evening do as well, which made it a long day. When I got home I could never let go of it. I had to sit down and watch the tapes through to make sure everything had come out all right. I'd stay up all night, looking through all the pictures. I think Julie had a job to live with me when I was doing those weddings. It was too nerve-racking. So I tried not to do any more of them, and concentrated on the wildlife

Ready to go with all my gear.

Wildlife on Exmoor – a robin on a gatepost that let me right up close; a stag amongst the sheep in winter, looking across the valleys of Exmoor. A squirrel, some frogs and the boar that roam wild on the moor.

Left: *With Bambi, who was poorly at the time.*

Below: *Introducing Tommy the buzzard to Bambi in the garden.*

Bottom: *Bambi when we first found her with an injured leg.*

Main photograph: *A badger grubbing for food.*

Inset: *Badgers on the 'assault course'.*

The deer of Exmoor, (clockwise): twin red deer calves in the spring; a huge stag, known as 'The Badgercombe Stag', roars in the mating season; stags and hinds after the rut; a herd of stags near Horsen.

Wild ponies on Exmoor.

Main photograph: *Searching for vipers in the heather.*

Inset: *A viper warns me off.*

Above: *My new hide in the bluebell wood.*

Below: *The view down from the hide's window.*

Right: *Filling the badger wheel with peanuts.*

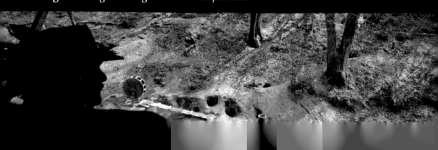

Main picture: *The graveyard where my parents and little Paul are buried.*

Inset: *Me with Paul before I left for the army. This was the last picture of him before he died.*

films. I expanded the areas I travelled to, and I worked out that I could maybe hope to make £50 a show, plus sell some of the tapes at £10 each. With maybe a couple of shows a week, and the gravedigging thrown in, I'd keep us going.

My friend Joe Drewer sometimes came with me when I was showing films, as well as my best mate Mike Warren. We thought it would be a good idea to travel to Blandford, to the great steam engine rally there – and stay for six nights. We decided to take with us a shed, which we could stack in sections in the rear of the Mazda pick-up. During the day we could use the shed as our stall, for setting out photographs and videos for sale, and so on, with a television inside actually showing the videos. At night, we'd roll out our sleeping bags and sleep on the floor. So Terry Saunders set to work and built this construction, which looked a bit like a wooden burger van, except that instead of selling burgers it sold videos and photographs of wildlife, and so on. He built it in five sections so it would bolt together easily enough, plus a ground sheet. For poor Joe Drewer, who'd been in the war, sleeping in that shed was like going back to his army days.

We went on the road. In between the filming and the gravedigging, travelling to agricultural shows with the shed became a way of life, and Julie started to come with me. She'd hold up the sections of shed – pretty difficult if there was a wind – so that I could line up the holes and slot the bolts in. It worked, but after a while we did try and think how we might improve the situation. It had become a bit of a nuisance, putting it up and taking it down all the time.

Joe walked in one day with a copy of the motoring section of *Exchange and Mart*. 'Look at this,' he said. I leaned over to take a look. He tapped with his forefinger. 'An old caravan chassis,' he said.

'So what?'

'Costs next to nothing. How about we get hold of it, tow it back here and bolt the shed on top of 'un?'

'What an idea.'

'Then we can tow the thing, and it's already up and ready to go.'

Joe and I went down to Cornwall and looked it over. It was a bit rusty, but it worked OK. We hauled it back to Bishop's Nympton and took it directly over to Kevin Boyle's place, and he did a terrific job fitting the shed on top of that chassis. For almost no money at all we'd turned an old shed into a fully operational towed vehicle. 'That's not a shed any more,' said Joe, 'it's a chariot.' And that's what it came to be known as: the chariot.

We wouldn't have to put it up and take it down ever again. That was luxury, just to roll into the showground or whatever, park up – and we were open for business straight off. The big fear was, of course, that some day

the whole thing would tear off the chassis and fly into the windscreen of the car following us, but Kevin had done it so well, you could tow the chariot at 60 mph without any problem. Today, as I write, it sits on a patch of ground opposite my house, retired from its duties.

This was our roadshow. When people visited the chariot they'd see a display of photographs, plus videos for sale, and the generator-powered television showing *A Life On Exmoor* or suchlike by Johnny Kingdom. At night the mattresses would come out and we'd sleep in there. You can imagine the times we had. Withycombe Fair was one of the best shows. We had adventures all over the place. Not all of them were good times, as you might imagine. Once Julie woke up in the middle of the night and needed water – I stumbled out and went to the boot of the car to get some. I grabbed a bottle and went back to the chariot and handed it to her. She took a swig and straightaway sprayed it all over me, choked and coughed and spluttered, her eyes watered, it was dreadful. I'd handed her a bottle of methylated spirits. Things like that you don't forget.

There you are, Johnny,' said Dr Chesterfield, 'you can use that old electricity pylon, down in the wood there.' Around that time the electricity company was pulling down a whole line of pylons, and several of the old ones were lying about. Farmers bought them and used the steel for various building projects. Dr Chesterfield was kindly suggesting that I could build a hide from which to photograph wildlife on his land. He lived not far from Bishop's Nympton, at South Hayne, with some 'off ground' at North Hayne. There was a little plot up there, covered with hazel and birch trees. There was no badger sett, so it would have to be a bird hide. I very quickly accepted his offer – this was exactly what I wanted.

I had a lot of help building the hide from friends and family. We carried a heavy old generator across three fields to bring power for the tools. We spent weeks cutting and unbolting that electricity pylon. So that was the structure – but what about the viewing platform? I needed timber, lots of it. At the time they were building the North Devon link road and I happened to spy a whole load of shuttering they were using to pour concrete into, to make a bridge. I went along and asked the foreman, 'What happens to all that board, once you're done with it?'

'Why d'you ask?' he said.

'I'm putting up a hide.'

'What for?'

'I want to film some birds. I'll make some nesting boxes with glass backs so I can film them hatch their young.' I told him I was using the old electricity pylon to build the frame. I just needed the wooden shuttering for the sides and platforms.

'Come back in a week's time,' he said. 'I'll see what I can do.'

He gave me as much as I could carry away, for nothing. All that board – it was amazing luck. This was some hide now – around eight by eight feet, no less than 26 feet high, all boarded in, with a roof. No more black plastic binbag to cover the camera. It took a whole gang of people from the village to put it up. It was a good laugh and I was proud that so many people wanted to help. It made me feel I was on the right track; it gave me a lot of determination. If they were going to give so much of their time and effort, then I was going to repay them with great results.

We had bird boxes countersunk into the hide. Each box had a square of plywood which could be raised to reveal a piece of glass, so that we could film what was going on right in the nesting box. Eventually the birds would get so used to us that we took the wood out, and it was a bit like being in the nest with them. We had blue tits, a tomtit or great tit, as it's known, a nuthatch – all sorts. A spotted flycatcher actually chose to fly into the hide and build its nest up above our heads, but we couldn't film it because there wasn't enough light up there.

Come November, we'd clean out the boxes and start again – wait and see what we'd get next year.

I filmed so many lovely sequences in that hide. My favourite was the pair of tawny owls who came back year after year, except for the one time the squirrels invaded and turfed out their nest. The answer to that was to make another box for the squirrels nearby so they moved in there, and then, the year after, I got my tawny owls back. Their chicks start out as just balls of fluff, tiny, but they grow out their feathers so quickly and then they are the prettiest sight. Those tawny owls are still there, after seventeen years, probably descendants of the original pair, although they do live a long time.

The hide is very wonky now, after so many years. I haven't been up there for a few months, but I still clean out the boxes every year, so they can keep going. That patch of land has changed hands three times, but always on condition that my hide remains there. I hope it keeps on.

I was excited by the pictures I was getting from those glass-backed bird boxes, but I wanted to have a hide from which to film badgers. It's one of the things I'm known for, my badgers, and, especially since you can only see them at night, I needed a badger hide.

Clifford Woollacott provided the answer. He lived up at Twitchen, and had a badger sett on a steep piece of ground, a cleave just up against the edge of a fir plantation. He very kindly gave me permission to build a hide there. Mike Warren – always my friend and my helper – was able to send some scaffold poles my way because the building regulations had been changed and these ones had become sub-standard and therefore couldn't be used. The structure I built was eight feet high – the length of the scaffold poles – and four by four feet square. The platform was made out of scaffold boards cut to size, but open to the weather. The whole thing was rigged with ropes to each corner to hold it down. It wasn't that well built; if there was any kind of wind it swayed around and generally gave the impression it was on the verge of collapse. Of course, badgers only come out at night, so I had to work out a way of getting some light that wouldn't put them off and yet would give me enough for the camera. This was before the days of infrared, mind. I set a light high up and pointed it at the sett, but then covered it with a red cloth. The idea was to get them used to the red light, and then slowly progress to yellow – and if I didn't turn it up too bright I was hoping they'd think it was the moon and not worry.

The sett was around 20 feet away, further up the slope. I sat out, that first night in my new hide, watching for them – which is some amount of waiting, let me tell you. But I didn't see anything. Perhaps it would take a while longer for them to get used to the presence of the hide. I gave it a while and then went back.

Another night – still nothing.

I waited a third night, but again I didn't see one. Not a peep. Something was wrong. The only thing I could think of was that they were smelling me. Badgers can't see very well, but they have an acute sense of smell. I'd thought I was high enough up for my scent to be carried away, but maybe not. There was only one way to find out – go higher. I went back to Mike Warren and he managed to kit me out with some more of that out-of-date scaffolding. I went up another six feet and put in a second platform.

Now things happened. I started to see badgers. It's amazing how that extra height meant they lost my scent. I got some great shots and was pleased as Punch. This was going to work.

Then I got ambitious. I needed to be a bit more canny about getting the shots that I knew my audiences wanted. Instead of waiting for things to happen, why not make them happen? My audience's *oohs* and *aahhhs* came when they saw something unusual, rather than a badger just walking along, or a bird just flying.

My thoughts went back to my childhood, and Uncle Bert making me a box to keep mice in. He'd made little runs and corridors, he'd put a bedroom for them up on another level, and he'd made a wheel for them to play on. Could I do something similar for my badgers?

First off, I thought, let's see them finding and eating food.

And so Julie made her first badger cake.

JULIE KINGDOM'S BADGER CAKE

½ lb of lard	Melt the lard in a big pan. Stir in the
Sugar Puffs	Sugar Puffs, sultanas and peanuts until
sultanas	the mixture is a sticky mess.
peanuts	Take off the heat, turn out into a greased
jam and honey	cake tin and leave to cool.
(optional)	Serve cold, buried underground.

If you follow the recipe you'll find out it's a fairly solid cake – not much to look at, not a cake you'd want to offer the vicar's wife on a Sunday afternoon, by any means. But we knew the badgers would love it. I went out to the hide and dug a little pit, and put the cake in and covered it with earth. When it was dark I went up to my platform and waited, camera ready. It was so exciting, truly it was, to see that badger come out, sniff around and make his way to where I'd buried the cake. He scratched away and in no time he'd dug up his cake and was eating it. I knew audiences would love that. It was such a pleasure to see. It filled me with satisfaction.

Next I went out and bought a flat microphone, which was basically a metal plate about six inches square attached to a long lead that went back to the camera. Julie made another badger cake and I took it and dug a deeper pit and put the microphone in the bottom of it, with the cake on top. Then I filled it in, climbed back in the hide and waited.

The badger came and dug up the cake, but this time there wasn't just the sight of him, we got the scratching of his paws and the snuffling and then the fantastic noise of his teeth mashing together, his chewing and swallowing – all amplified I don't know how many times. What a racket! It brought the whole thing much closer; it was like it was happening right bang in front of our eyes.

Time went on. I had quite a few visitors at the hide. Julie doesn't like heights, but she came. Her friend Sally, too, although she stayed down the bottom as she didn't like the look of the platform 12 feet up. Any amount of people from the village came. We had some good nights up there in that hide.

Then came the news that Clifford Woollacott was going to retire. It was a sad day, taking it down. Damn, I thought, as we worked away – what wouldn't I give for a bit of land of my own? We're very lucky hereabouts in that Exmoor is a National Park and anyone has the right to roam over it at will, but it would be a nice thing to have a piece of ground of my own, where I wouldn't be disturbed.

Eventually I got some good news: Terry and Carol Rudd gave me permission to build a hide on Aller Farm. It was Mike Warren, again, who gave me so much help, along with the late Joe Drewer. We had to dig out a flat base because the ground was steep. We'd salvaged the scaffold poles from the hide up at Clifford's place and now we could use them again, plus more that Mike managed to bring. This was a bigger and better hide altogether. It had a roof and was weatherproof. We made some bird feeders too – there was a big old ash tree nearby and we strung a washing line between the hide and the tree, around 10 feet off the ground, and hung the feeders on there, which allowed us to film the woodpeckers and all sorts who came to visit.

Now I could get going again, and build my badger playground. We were going to have some fun, to play games with them, tease them with all sorts of things. They are such lovable and comical creatures.

First we got hold of a long pipe and ran it from the top of the hide down to the ground near the sett. Badgers are very curious, so of course they came to have a look at it. As they sniffed their end of it, we rolled a nut down. They jumped out of their skins; they couldn't understand it. And then of course they got the hang of it, so they'd gather round and stare at this magic pipe, waiting for the next nut to roll down.

We put an egg out for them, to see what they'd do. Just a single egg, down on the ground, as if it had dropped from the sky. A group of youngsters, half grown, saw this strange and frightening object. They approached with great caution, an inch at a time. When they got close enough to see just how awful it was, their courage deserted them and they turned and ran. This happened five or six times. And then a full-grown badger came and showed them what was what. She walked up to the egg and picked it up in her mouth, delicate as you like. She held up her nose, ran 10 yards and took it back down the hole to eat it, without a second thought. It does prove that badgers take eggs, when they find them.

We sank a drainage pipe into the earth so that it stuck up around 15 inches above ground. Then we filled it with peanuts. This was so we could film the badgers standing up on their back legs and hooking out the nuts with their paws. Next we nailed a platform together, around two feet square, with a ladder going up to it. In the middle of the platform we bolted a stool, with a pipe in the seat of it. After a while the badgers learned to climb the ladder, hop on to the stool and hook out the nuts and the honey in the pipe. All this made for more entertaining footage. Our badgers didn't know it, but they were becoming good performers. We added more to the circuit: another ladder, more platforms, narrow walkways.

The mice I'd kept when I was a boy had enjoyed turning their wheels – why not see if the badgers would like a wheel of their own, a badger-sized one? I was keen to try it out and talked to Gordon Parker about it, with a view that he might make one for me. He listened to the idea, and although he was sceptical he agreed to help.

There was one farmer who said, 'If Johnny Kingdom thinks badgers are going to turn that wheel then he's off his rocker.'

We had the wheel fixed in place, we put honey on it – and the badgers thought it was a great game to get the honey off. A swarm of bees thought so, too, once. We built a second wheel. And we went down the local pub and got an aluminium beer barrel and painted it green. I had all sorts of things going on – the big badgers turning the big wheel and the cubs turning the beer barrel. We tried different inventions. We put a drum in the middle of the wheel with holes drilled into it, so that nuts would fall out when they spun it round. It was a regular assault course and amusement park, for badgers.

As well as the films I made, there were the visitors who came out to see for themselves what was going on. The Bishop's Nympton women's skittle team came one night. Bloody hell, I had to be strict with them. The smoking, the perfume, the wine, the talking! What chance would there be of seeing anything that night? The girls were spread out over the four different levels in the hide, waiting. Luckily the wind was in the right direction and they had a wonderful night, truly magical.

The badger sett grew. Our feeding them allowed for a greater population. It went from four holes to six in the first twelve months.

We had years of pleasure from that hide, and I got

some great shots to go in my films. I remember we had one particular badger called Snowy, because he was like an albino, near enough white all over.

And then came foot and mouth. After years of nuts and honey and fun and games, all sorts of visitors, suddenly the badgers were on their own. We couldn't go anywhere near. On top of that, the bottom cover, which was on the way to the hide, was sold. A padlock went on the gate, so we no longer had access to it. The hide had to come down. Half the village turned up to help dismantle everything and load it on to the tractor and trailer and haul it away: Richard Jennings, Mike Warren, my boys, Frankie Hooper, Paul and Robert Kingdon, Joe Drewer, Steve Govier. Tony Thorne (no relation to the other Thornes in this book) brought his tractor along to help. We attached a rope to the top of the construction and tried pulling it over, but the rope kept on breaking. Or the tractor would lift off the ground. It was a hell of a job, but we got it done.

It was the end of an era.

But Tony Thorne not only brought his tractor along. He offered another kind of help. He gave the hide a new home, at his place up at Twitchen, Higher House Farm. It's still there today. I thank you, Tony Thorne.

As well as the badgers and the birds, I kept up my stalking and photographing of red deer. I was putting together a film I would call *The Rutting Stags of Exmoor*. Up near White Chapple, in a lovely spot in a wooded valley, I'd been lucky enough to find a deer-wallow under an oak tree – that's to say, a place where the deer would go to splash and roll in the mud, give themselves a bath. I wanted to try and film this happening, close up. Deer are such flighty creatures – one scent or sound will set them off. And because they are particularly vulnerable when they're wallowing, they'd be making double sure they were safe. I'd have to be well hidden to catch them at it.

For four days on the trot I went up there early in the morning and waited, and waited. I was camouflaged and downwind of the wallow, but I saw nothing. Somehow the deer were getting wind of me and staying away.

On the fifth day I went even earlier, when it was still dark, around four in the morning. I took no torch, but made my way through the pitch black, my camera and some sandwiches and a flask in a rucksack as usual. An Exmoor wood in the middle of the night is a spooky place to be. I found my way to the wallow and climbed the tree, up into its branches. There I settled down to wait. I heard a tawny owl calling, which scared me. I heard a stag roar, not very far off. For four hours I sat on that branch, leaning against the trunk. I grew very stiff and numb.

Inch by inch, it grew light. I held my breath. If it was going to happen at all, it would be now.

Then, around eight thirty in the morning, twelve deer – hinds and yearlings – quietly picked their way through the woodland, walking with such perfect grace and quietness as took your breath away. A hind stepped into the wallow right beneath where I was sitting and daintily sat down in the mud. She lay right out on her side, then rolled on her back and kicked her legs in the air. From above, I filmed her – I was almost shaking with excitement. She rolled from side to side, over and over. Then she picked herself up, shook the mud off her coat, and stepped out.

Then it was the turn of the next one. She stepped into the wallow, sank to her knees, and rolled on to her side. Likewise, she kicked her legs up, rolled back and forth. It was an incredible sight.

A little calf came next; I could look down on its back and count the white spots. She'd learned from her mum what to do.

I filmed all twelve of that herd of deer as, one by one, they used the wallow. Even the calves – they all wallowed. I was over the moon.

Last of all came the stag. He was a beauty. This was breathtaking – a royal stag, brow, bay, tray and three on top – the Queen's deer. This naming of the deer as 'royal' came from the times when Exmoor had been what they

called a 'royal forest' – huge areas of the country were set aside for use by the monarch for hunting, and it was forbidden for anyone else to use them.

This stag had obviously been keeping a look-out, and now it was his turn. He was extremely suspicious. He stood right under my tree and sniffed the ground. He was uneasy, but he couldn't quite put his finger on what was wrong. He looked in all directions, he tested the air. But he couldn't find anything. So he decided to take his bath. He rolled in the wallow, just as his herd had done.

He stood up, shook off the mud and waited. There was still something bothering him, you could see him trying to work it out.

Then he looked up. Through the lens of the camera I met his eye. He was looking at a man, his sworn enemy, his predator, right above him.

The instant he saw me he bolted – and his herd with him. There was no more than a couple of seconds of the sound of their crashing through undergrowth, and then silence, as if nothing had happened.

You can imagine how tired and excited and amazed I was as I put my camera and my Thermos and the wrappings from my sandwiches in the backpack, and climbed down out of that tree, sore as hell. I had enough aches and pains to last for weeks, but it was the best footage I was ever to get of Exmoor's red deer.

There is a postscript to that story. It so happened that

there was an application made to turn that area of land into a golf course and leisure centre. There were those who were for this development, and those of us who didn't want it. Things went so high up that a government minister became involved. They showed the minister my film of those deer wallowing as part of the argument against the development.

The minister decided against the golf course. The deer-wallow is still there.

I wasn't the wild man any more, but I still enjoyed a good night out. In 1988 Julie and I celebrated our twenty-fifth wedding anniversary, and that was a night to remember. It was Ron Disborough's birthday, too, which added to the mayhem. Lynsey and Teresa Chilcott had given me a pair of braces with the words 'Rock on Tommy' printed on them. The do was held at the Black Cock and everyone was there – both sons, all our mates. Roger Gregory filmed it for posterity. I drank a lot of cider. A lot, mind. And then came the whisky chasers. Oh, my Lord. I put my whisky glass down so hard it bounced out of my hand and all down the bar. There was music and dancing and since I seemed to have lost my whisky glass I took to dancing. I poked my thumbs under the braces and did a series of great dance moves, but it didn't end up too well.

The braces got caught up over my head. I was in knots, hanged up in my own braces. There were roars of laughter from the crowd, which was enough for me to want to carry on anyway, tied up or no.

I can't remember coming home that night, but there is photographic evidence. They got me back to Bishop's Nympton, and they hauled me upstairs. They laid me on the bed, mouth open, snoring away, in a shocking state. A Worzel Gummidge doll lived on our pillow and they pushed that snug up against me. After that, they unlocked the gun cabinet and took out two rifles and a twelve-bore shotgun and propped them up next to me on the bed and wrapped my arms round them so I looked like an old gunslinger from the Wild West. Roger Gregory – he who'd lent me the camera that time – filmed it all, just for the record. Twenty-five years of marriage and look what Julie found in her bed.

Overnight success

" Then a big sturdy man walked past, and he stopped to have a look . . . **"**

had made three films, *Wildlife on Exmoor*, *The Rutting Stags of Exmoor* and *Gateway to Exmoor*. I had hauled myself out of trouble. I was set on a course now; I had the life I wanted. If enough people bought my videos I could carry on. I was a changed man, and a better one.

In 1992 I was at Honiton Show, selling my videos and photographs as usual in the chariot. I'd had fifteen years of experience at this game. It was business as usual.

Then a big sturdy man walked past, and he stopped to have a look, as people do. He introduced himself as Willie Poole. He was round-faced, a working man, perhaps he came from Scotland, one might guess. He wore a big gentleman's top hat – he was there with a pack of hounds in some capacity or other. Anyway, he looked over my stuff and watched the film for a while. It turned out he was a journalist for the *Daily Telegraph* and he took away a couple of films with him. I thought nothing more of it.

The next I knew, he'd written to me saying he

thought *The Rutting Stags* was a 'masterpiece'. And, he went on, 'I'm going to put an article in the *Daily Telegraph* which will set you off, which you deserve.'

And so he did. The article appeared and I was pleased as Punch. This is what he wrote:

It has to be said that the videos lack a certain slickness in presentation. [Too right, I say, what an understatement, it was me and my finger on the pause button.] Mr Kingdom is his own production team; he works alone with a hand-held camcorder. [Yes, bloody hours of waiting, don't forget the waiting.] Some of his cutting is eccentric and the soundtrack occasionally develops background noise. [That's the sound of me cursing when I drop the camera in the mud.] But any technical shortcomings are more than compensated for by the sheer breathtaking skill of Mr Kingdom as a stalker and his deep knowledge of the countryside and all that is in it. [That's my favourite bit.] His commentary is unscripted and spontaneous and is conducted in deepest Devonian, which adds to the charm. The red deer are one of the glories of Exmoor and they make frequent appearances in wildlife films, but *Rutting Stags of Exmoor* is a masterpiece. It contains some of the finest film of deer that I have seen; shots that must have involved great

> skill, patience, discomfort and not a
> little personal risk: a stag maddened
> with lust is *dangerous*. I could babble
> on about the wonderful scenes - the
> deer-wallow, the fight in the thicket
> - ['I in't goin' in there!'] but I'll leave you
> to buy the film and watch and
> wonder . . .

You can imagine how proud I was at his words. They meant so much to me.

I'd hardly finished reading the article when the phone went. It was a man who introduced himself as James Cutler, who'd also read it. He was a director at Yorkshire Television, and he asked to meet me. He drove down from Yorkshire and parked his Volvo car outside my door in Bishop's Nympton. He was tall, six feet-odd, with dark, swept-back hair and glasses. He said he'd like to direct a film about me and my life on Exmoor. He offered me £7,000.

After he'd gone, Julie and I didn't quite know what to do with ourselves. This was the most extraordinary set of circumstances. Try as you might to think that life should carry on as normal, it didn't seem that it would. Suddenly we were thrown into the middle of this process of making a documentary film. Things moved so fast. Six weeks later we were making it, with cameraman Mostafa Hammuri. They took me to all my favourite spots on the moor, the places that meant the most to me, and I talked about my way of life – what I thought, what had happened. This wasn't just me and my camera, which I was used to. This was a whole production team, a big circus following me round: a director, a cameraman, a sound man, a producer, the assistants and drivers, and so on.

In a matter of months, with just two or three conversations, a phone call and a visit, it seemed as if my life had changed for ever. Neither Julie nor I could take it in.

James Cutler invited Julie and me up to Yorkshire, so we could look at the film being edited. This was a far cry from me and my finger on the pause button of the video player. They'd used proper film, which you cut with scissors and splice together with Sellotape – the old-fashioned but expensive way. It was very interesting to have a go. We stayed the night with the cameraman, Mostafa.

The film would be called *The Secret of Happiness*, and it was broadcast as part of ITV's 'First Tuesday' series on 2 November 1993, the same year my son Stuart and his girlfriend Sue got married.

We watched the programme with a lot of people from the village, in a pub called the Old Snare and Gin Trap. It was a big night. Everyone was drinking merrily, the TV was warmed up and chairs were put out. I had more drink than you could look at. I leaned up against the door frame at the back, glugging down a bottle of champagne that someone had bought me. The kids were at the front, sitting down. The programme came on and there was loud cheering. I found it very difficult. I was very emotional. Yes, it was a triumph, it was a big thing, but somehow it was like it was happening to someone else. It didn't seem like real life. Julie felt the same. It had all happened so quick.

It was a very late night and no doubt I was very drunk by the end of it. Somehow we got home.

The next day all hell let loose. The phone started ringing at eight in the morning and didn't stop – literally. You put the phone down and it rang in your hand immediately. We had to take it off the hook and give ourselves a half-hour break at lunch time. It only stopped ringing at ten o'clock that night. Stuart and Susan and me and Julie turned our front room into an office and post room. We swapped jobs. When your ear grew too hot from holding the phone for so long you changed to filling envelopes. When the taste of the stamps on your tongue became unbearable, you had a go on the phone. And so it went on, all day.

We filled 447 envelopes with copies of tapes. The next day fifty letters arrived in the post. Over the next three months we'd get 4,000 letters. We sold 7,000 tapes. In just three months £26,000 poured into our bank account. Daihatsu gave me a sponsored vehicle for a year. It was crazy.

I had another visit around that time. There was a

knock at my door – I wasn't expecting anyone. A man stood there, short with a big moustache. 'I've come to see you,' he said. 'My name is Sir John Harvey-Jones.'

It was obvious that I should know who he was, but I didn't. 'I'm sorry,' I replied, 'but I don't know you, sir.'

'Course you do,' hissed Julie, 'you know, that programme, what's it called, *Trouble Shooters*, is it?' I didn't know, but never mind. I wanted to hear what this fellow had to say.

'I've come to warn you, Johnny,' he said.

'Why, what's the problem?' I asked.

He replied very gravely, 'You've now joined the land of the sharks.' He went on to say that if ever I needed his help, I was to call him.

These were amazing times in the Kingdom household. We felt like we'd been tipped out of our old life and into a new one. I was on *Good Morning with Anne and Nick* at BBC Pebble Mill. I helped launch *Nature Detectives*. I was invited to open garden centres, visit schools. I opened the new Tarka the Otter train station in Bideford.

I was invited to be a guest speaker at the Ladies' Annual Skittle Dinner in South Molton. All the local ladies' skittle teams were there. I was sat next to the chairwoman, Sheila Philips, at the top table. I rose to my feet after having enjoyed my dinner and a few too many drinks. 'Ladies and gentlemen,' I began, and no doubt the words came a bit too thickly. I was swaying as well. 'I'd like to welcome you all,' I struggled on, 'this evening ...' and then I sat down in the chairwoman's lap.

Julie wasn't pleased. You can see her in the photograph, turning away; I'd let her down.

Slowly but surely the interest I'd received tailed off. I never called John Harvey-Jones, and I don't know that it was a world of sharks, exactly, that I found myself in, but it's true to say that I didn't know how to make the most of what had happened. I didn't have the business experience or the instinct for it. I should have got myself a TV agent, for instance, but I didn't. Within three months the phone calls began to die off, and almost as quick as we'd been picked up we were put down again, back in our ordinary lives. Never mind, I thought. That was fun. Carry on.

I was driving along one day, when I came round the corner and saw a stoat in the road – an unusual sight. I stopped the car, backed up and went and hid in the hedge with my camera, which I always carried with me. I was completely masked by undergrowth – invisible.

I waited.

The stoat reappeared. Then came another, and another. Four of them, playing in the road, tossing a stick about like a gang of kids. It's rare footage, wonderful. Wildlife photography is all about finding your luck and being ready to take it when it comes. In fact, I went on to get more stoat footage. I was called by Evelyn Pugsley and her husband, Wallace, retired farmers near South Molton, who told me they'd seen stoats playing in their garden in the very early morning. This was priceless. I went over and set up a camera in their kitchen and left it on the tripod, ready to go. They only had to switch it on for me. The legs of the tripod interfered with their cooker and they wouldn't be able to cook Sunday lunch, but they were determined to help. 'Never mind, Johnny,' said Evelyn, 'we'll use the microwave.' And they got some wonderful pictures for me.

This was my real life, what I was all about. And that hadn't changed. I was still going strong. It was like I'd been put back down in the place I loved most.

Bambi

" I took Bambi to the surgery right
there and then. **"**

In 1994 I got a phone call from Brian Buckingham, up at Polworthy Farm on the top of the moor. He'd gone out to see his sheep one morning and had found a red deer calf, only two or three days old, hung up in a fence. Her mother had jumped over to reach fresh young grass on the other side and this calf had tried to follow but had got her back leg caught. It was a pitiful sight, this beautiful baby with a shower of white spots over her back, obviously in pain and distressed, abandoned by her mother. Brian went back to fetch wire cutters and cut the calf free. She was so pretty, and so young, he didn't have the heart to kill her. Instead he took her back to his buildings and put her to rest in a shed, where she limped around, carrying her damaged leg. He knew how much I loved red deer, and how I was always looking after this or that animal in one way or another, and he called me that same night. 'Johnny,' he said, 'I've got this calf. I'm not sure she's going to live, she's got one foot badly damaged, but it occurred to me you might like to have a look at her, so we can decide what can be done.'

I was up there so early the next morning they were still in bed. Brian took me in the shed where this abandoned fawn trembled and limped around. The wire had marked her leg badly just above the hoof; it was serious.

I took her home with me there and then. It was heartbreaking – she was very stressed by the injury and the travelling, and with having lost her mother.

It wasn't surprising that we called her Bambi.

Julie and I took Bambi down to the vet's, where she was seen by Martin Prior. His expression told me it was bad. He gave me some powders for her.

I also faced an immediate problem: what could I feed her? Ordinary milk wouldn't do. It had to be sheep or goat's milk. I knew a woman named Jill Woollacott, who as it happened would marry my friend Mike Warren, and she kept goats. She agreed to provide Bambi with milk. So every day I went up there and brought the milk home for Bambi.

Of course this little calf had hardly known her mother. And because I slept out with her, and fed her, and carried her back and forth, in effect I became her mother. She bonded with me in that way. She came to me for comfort, for food, for safety.

After fourteen days her leg was no better. I called

Martin Prior. He came out straight away. 'That's not good,' he said. 'The foot is dead. And gangrene is spreading up her leg. We have to move quick.'

Amputation was the only answer. Martin gave Bambi only a fifty–fifty chance of survival. She wasn't even three weeks old. Our hearts were in our mouths.

I took Bambi to the surgery right there and then. That same afternoon Martin called me to say the operation had gone off as well as could be hoped. Bambi had come round.

But . . . she was calling for her mum.

Julie drove me into South Molton. The wound was terrible to look at, enough to make you flinch. To see a gash like that on such a young animal broke your heart.

I lay down beside Bambi in her kennel and put my arms around her. We stayed just like that for a bit, while Julie and the vet and I talked about what had happened, our hopes for her recovery, how we might look after her.

Bambi knew her mum had come for her. She stopped trembling and calmed down; she became quiet.

Then we took her home. She had to be fed every three hours, through the night. This was an intensive operation and Julie and I couldn't do it alone. It was the start of many wonderful, kind people coming to the house to help us with Bambi. I had a little granddaughter by this time, Roxy, and of course she fell in love with Bambi and helped me a lot with feeding. Bambi became a little better every day. After fourteen days the stitches came out. She was on the mend.

And of course I filmed all this. There are two complete Bambi videos. I've got footage of Martin Prior coming to take her stitches out and being so pleased with how the wound had healed, and of Bambi and me mucking around, wrestling together, and of her racing around the garden like it's a racecourse, and Bambi boxing with a bale of hay.

She became part of the family. We made a pen for her in the back garden and it was comical to see her running around on her three legs. There was a sacrifice to be made – Julie had to lose most of her garden, and Bambi ate her roses. We had a lead for her, and a collar; she was one of our pets, along with Sandy the lurcher, and Spotty, the Jack Russell who came to us smaller than the palm of your hand, and Garfield, an allsorts dog, who liked to chase the shadows when you shone the torch, and of course the cat, Smoky. They're all buried in the garden now – Bambi survived them all.

I had another granddaughter not long afterwards – Louise – and she loved Bambi just like Roxy did. Joe Drewer, his wife Rene and their daughter Angela came down countless times to look after her, feed her, and so on. Joe's passed away now and is much missed; I had the privilege of burying him myself. He used to keep the tops of cabbages and carrots for Bambi to eat. Adrian and Carol Adams and their kids came a lot to visit her and help with her care. And Michael Warren's daughter Lynda and her partner Justin, and their daughters Jodie and Milly helped when we were away. And of course Bambi's famous among the people who've seen her films. It's generally known amongst her fans that she likes custard cream biscuits, and many's the time I've come home to find a package on the doorstep or in the garage with a note 'Custard Creams for Bambi'.

She still treats me as her mother. I had a buzzard living in the house recently and Bambi was dead jealous of that bird. She freezes me out if I cause her any trouble. She calls for me if I'm not there – 'Mrrrrrr!' Then she calms down when I appear. She doesn't like it when I trim her feet with secateurs, and bites me on the head. That's the reason I'm going bald, I always say. It's a father–daughter relationship.

Recently she took very ill, and a man called Tony Nevin came to see her. He's an animal osteopath, and after he'd laid his hands on her in different places she shook out her fur in a way that she hadn't done for a few months, which told me that he'd done her a lot of good, without question. Of course with Bambi's back leg missing she's got all the weight on the one joint, and she's finding it hard to walk now that she's getting older. But she looks so well that I want to give her every chance. She's twelve years old, and the day will come – not too far away now – when we lose her, I know that, but it will be such a sad day.*

I had followed my father into the gravedigging business, and sure enough, in their turn, my sons joined me. Craig was fourteen when we went to work in the little village of Westleigh, near Instow, a beautiful place looking down on the estuary. It wasn't our usual undertaker, it was a new one from Barnstaple, so it wasn't a graveyard we were familiar with.

*Postscript – as I put the finishing touches to this book, on 31 July, 2006, I'm sad to say that Bambi had to be put to sleep. I'd like to thank Martin Prior, the vet, for being so kind to her throughout her life. She could no longer stand up; it was the saddest sight. The very next day, when I went into South Molton, no fewer than nine people came up to me, who'd already heard. Flowers have started to arrive for her. She will always be in our hearts, and she is now resting in peace.

I started to dig and noticed immediately that the ground was very soft. This was good news in one way, because it meant easy work and we'd be done with quicker. But there was always a danger with very soft ground that the sides of the grave would collapse. This had happened to me before – I'd been six feet down and the entire side came in. I'd been hit on the head by a stone – all sorts. I'd been lucky to get out; to be nearly buried alive is not a pleasant experience.

Craig and I went to work. We took off the clats and laid them to one side to be replaced later. I dug down the first two feet very easily. When I'd reached halfway, three feet down, I said to Craig, 'right, it's your turn.' I climbed out and he hopped in and took over the digging while I watched. 'Be very careful,' I warned him, 'of that right-hand side. Don't undercut 'un. It's ready to fall if you do.' Down he went. I was above him, looking down on his back as he was bent over, digging, so I saw what happened, but he didn't. There was a sudden give in that right-hand side, but it wasn't earth, it was slats of old rotten timber that spilled out – a coffin had burst on that side, at the same height as Craig's head. Out of the coffin rolled a complete skull, and hit craig on his shoulder. He jumped – and the skull rolled over his shoulder and dropped right in front of him – *thud*. Worse was to come: all its teeth fell out. This happened in an instant, and at the same time Craig gave a great big shout. I've never seen anyone jump out of a hole in the ground so quick. He was white as milk and shaking, poor lad, and it was a while before he could laugh at it.

It makes you wonder who that man was, what he'd done during his life. It reminds you that you can't tell where you'll end up, nor what will happen to you, even when you're in your grave. I bet that person would never have guessed, not in a million years, that their skull was going to roll over the shoulder of a young lad in the last decade of the twentieth century, and all their teeth would fall out and frighten him half to death.

That coffin had burst open because the ground was soft. In the graveyard at Bishop's Nympton the ground was harder and stonier, and graves took a lot longer to dig. I worked a lot up there with a man who lived near us. Both he and his wife were friends of ours. Julie was particularly fond of him. This man was in the grave, scratching away, when I came to the conclusion that he wasn't himself. He was worried about something. 'You all right?' I called to him. 'Yup,' came the answer, but I could tell from his tone the opposite was true. 'What is it?' I went on.

'Oh, nothing.'

I pressed him. 'Go on, you can tell me.'

'Well . . . no, I won't tell you now, not here.'

'Why on earth not?'

'You might clout me on the back of the head with a shovel if I tell you when I'm down here,' he said.

Well, this was odd. What could it be that would make me want to do such a thing? I couldn't think. It was a puzzle.

'OK, you get out and I'll get in and dig, and then you can tell me,' I said. And so we did. We swapped round and I was in the grave, and he was above. 'So you can tell me now,' I told him. And I made a guess. 'Have you got someone else, is that it?'

There was a pause then, which told me I'd hit the mark. 'Yes,' he said, 'there is.' And of course I was thinking that Julie liked this man quite a lot and that if there'd been any reason I'd want to hit him with a shovel ... 'do I know her?' I asked. My stomach was ready to turn a somersault.

'No, you wouldn't know her – because he's called Stephen.'

Well, I'm blowed, I thought. That came as a bolt out of the blue. But things turned out all right. As he said at the time, 'I just found someone, Johnny, who loves me.' He left his wife and went to live with Stephen and they are still together to this day.

I said to my wife, 'Julie, can you come over here and look at my backside?' It's the sort of thing you can say to a wife, but even so this wasn't going to be pleasant for her.

'Why, John, what's wrong?'

'It feels like all my innards are coming out and it's sore as hell.'

She had a look. 'Oh, John, you've got piles.' She tried not to laugh.

I went to the doctor and there was more embarrassment. He prescribed some injections to try and make these things go away. This went on for about a year. They were tremendously painful and I didn't like it one bit. The long and short of it was, these piles – like a bunch of grapes hanging out my backside – refused to lie back down. We had to admit defeat. They sent me to the hospital in Ilfracombe.

To put it bluntly, the operation to cure piles involves stretching your backside wide as a garage. God knows what implement they use. The mind boggles at the idea of what that looks like, for the surgeon. When I came round from the operation I could hardly walk. The only way I could move from one spot to another was very slowly, with this stiff, bow-legged gait, like a zombie cowboy.

Around teatime Julie came to pick me up. I don't know what she was thinking of, but she'd brought along a friend of hers, Sally, so that she could witness my humiliation too. What was worse, she'd turned up in the tiniest little car you could imagine, a Mini. It was not funny, trying to get into that car. Half bent over, I tried to go in front ways. Hanging off the roof, I had a stab at going in backwards. All the time this grimace of agony was on my face. Eventually I got into that Mini on my knees. It wasn't funny, but they couldn't stop laughing.

There are some people who seem to go through life without having to deal much with hospitals, but it seems our God has seen fit to land me with quite a few injuries and illnesses. The injuries have mostly been to do with motor vehicles, and the illnesses have mostly been of the embarrassing sort. If I say the words 'barium meal enema' I can make Julie smile, even after forty-three years of marriage, so I suppose it has its uses. I had polyps in my innards and they wanted to check what was going on. They put you in a gown which ties up at the back, which is the first thing to make you look silly, and the next thing is they put a bath hat on your head. Then they make you carry your clothes in a basket to the ward, where there are a load of other people who know what's going on. Julie was already laughing at me then.

They put me on the bed, hoisted me in the air, stuck a tube up my backside and pumped me full of barium meal – still while I was wearing this gown and hat. There was a pretty young nurse helping me, which made it worse. She turned me in all directions while they took the X-rays, still with the tube in – agony it was. Then I was asked to get off my bed, still with this tube in, except now it was connected to a bag carried by the lovely nurse, and the idea was, as politely as possible, for her to get all the barium meal out, the same way it went in. She very kindly walked my tube and my bag and me, wearing my funny hat and gown, all the way to the bathroom, where she backed me up to the toilet bowl. When I was ready she pulled the plug, as it were, and the tube came out of my backside. She strongly advised me to stay there for at least fifteen minutes. There came, then, the most Godawful series of violent noises and explosions from my backside – it was enough to make my eyes water. I was left looking at a huge mountain of a blancmange-type stuff rising out of the toilet – shameful it was, really. The worst of it was having to wear that nightgown tied up at the back, and the silly hat.

You cannot escape from an experience like that with your dignity. You just cannot.

And perhaps now is the time to admit that when I was nineteen, and had just gone up to Shropshire for my basic training, I had to have an operation to sort out a varicose problem in my genitals. After the operation, my meat and two veg were so badly swollen they had to be strapped up in a bag. The pain was terrible, the sight of them was awful. They swelled up so large. The pain was worse if they were allowed to hang down, so I had to keep them held up somehow. The nurses searched their cupboards for a big enough bag to keep them tied up in, but there wasn't one. I had to walk back and forth to the toilets trying out all these different sizes of bags, so the other men in the ward laughed like hell. But I had to have a bag of some sort, I couldn't walk around all day holding them up myself – too heavy, for a start. A very kind old lady came to the rescue. She was over eighty years old but she set to work, and she knitted me a bag out of coloured wool. It was crochet, technically speaking. That is not a word of a lie: I was carrying my own genitals around in a crocheted bag made for me by an old lady. It's not something to fill a young man with confidence, let me tell you.

I always enjoyed my football and managed the Bishop's Nympton B side for some years. It was great fun: there was plenty of cider and laughs. My mate Keith Setherton was the boss of the A team and ran the whole thing, and so when we opened the door of the van and mooned the residents of South Molton, it was him we had to answer to. We agreed to moderate our behaviour. But there was always singing and a bit of scandal and those kinds of goings-on around the football teams. We weren't that good, for the most part – we lost 18–1 on one occasion. That was more like a rugby score. The height of my football achievements was when I was playing for the first team and we won the YMCA cup against Landkey, 1–0.

My cousin Terry scored the goal. That was some celebration, that night, down the Bish Mill pub. I ended up standing on a chair on top of a table and singing, 'Eee iii add-ee-oh, we won the cup,' and then I put my fist through the ceiling.

That was the best, but perhaps the low point was when we played against Bideford. I'd parked on the harbour front there. A few feet in front of us there was a straight drop into the sea. Julie and I came out of the pub and we got into the car. She said, 'For God's sake, make sure you go backwards, John, not forwards.' She was right to mention it, because while we were in the pub the tide had gone out and so there was a 20-foot drop just a few feet ahead of us. 'Don't be so bluddy silly,' I swore, ''course I'm going to go backwards. What am I, mad?' I put the Allegro into gear, looked over my shoulder and let the clutch in.

The car leapt forwards.

Julie screamed. We were heading straight over the sea wall. I'd had a drink or two and my feet and hands were all over the place . . .

It was our fantastic luck that the car went up on a mooring, an iron plug around 15 inches high that the boats tied their ropes to – otherwise we could have been killed. The Allegro climbed up on to this mooring and got stuck, its front wheels off the ground.

It can be imagined how angry Julie was with me. I think the word divorce was mentioned. She's earned

quite a few medals for patience and forgiveness during our marriage. She went back to the pub and fetched the football team. They all came out and had their laugh, and then lifted the Allegro off the mooring and put it back down, and we drove home.

Things weren't too good between my wife and me for a day or two after that. I can still feel a cold chill round the back of my neck, just remembering it.

The buzzard is a very shy creature, like the deer. You can only dream about capturing buzzards close up on film. You can be driving along and see one perched on a telegraph pole, but as soon as you stop and look at him, he's off. They have very good eyesight and an almost supernatural ability to detect movement.

I was lucky enough to spot a buzzard's nest in a beech tree not far from the Black Cock Inn, a pub I often go to. I saw him come out from his nest – this was rare. I climbed the tree – high, mind, 25 or 30 feet up. But there were plenty of branches and that made it quite easy. When I was about halfway up the buzzard flew off, high in the sky, and started calling. I went on up, until I was in a position to look down into the nest. I knew there was a risk of putting the parents off their work, but I hoped and prayed I wouldn't do so.

The buzzard builds quite a big, untidy nest, without much in the way of lining – no feathers or wool for comfort or warmth, just maybe some fine grasses at the bottom. This one was big enough to sit in, maybe three feet across, and in the middle were two large eggs. It was a lovely sight. Also littering the nest was part of a rabbit, a couple of magpie's wings and a lamb's tail – evidence of the adults' last few meals. I filmed the two eggs and then put the camera back in the haversack and climbed down. If I could come back regularly, maybe I'd see the eggs hatch.

I visited the nest again three days later. As I approached, the parent bird flew out, so that was good – I hadn't scared them off. This time it was a more hair-raising climb because a terrific wind was blowing and the higher I went, the more slender were the branches and the more they waved about, as if this old beech tree was trying to throw me off. I clung on and reached my position, and looked down into the nest.

There was only one egg in there. Alongside it was a little white ball of fluff – a buzzard chick. One born, one still to go.

It was the cutest little thing, like out of a children's storybook – a ball of fluff with a beak and two eyes. I filmed it quickly – I didn't want to stay long.

Every few days I climbed up to that nest, hung up my haversack on the same branch and filmed the buzzard family. The second egg never did hatch, so there was just the one baby that I watched grow. He lost the perfect whiteness of his fluffy coat. First there were hints of brown at the tips of his feathers, and gradually they darkened. He grew fast – a buzzard is a very big bird, so he had a hell of a way to go and not much time to do it in. He ate up everything he was given. He flapped his little baby wings and looked out over the terrain. He called for his mum and dad. More and more bits of litter appeared in the nest – bones, fur, old card and string.

The parents grew quite used to me. They'd fly off to a neighbouring tree and watch me, making their anxious *peeeowww* sound, and then they'd return after I'd gone.

I kept going every few days, until the chick was a full-size fledgling. So quick, like magic, he'd grown. Once, he edged out of the nest and on to the nearest branch. He spread his wings right out, then closed them again. I held my breath – that was some sight. He was practising, with that enormous pair of wings grown in such a short time. It was so exciting to see. He opened them again and flapped them a few times. He was trying them for size.

And then he dropped off the branch and flew.

He swooped over the valley and landed a bit clumsily in the first tree he could find. It took my breath away, that did. And I had it all on film.

I'm too old now to risk my neck climbing trees, but I'm so proud to have got this kind of shot so that people can see these rare sights for themselves. In fact, only a few months ago I got some more very unusual footage of a buzzard, but I didn't have to risk my neck climbing trees in the wind and rain to get it; instead the buzzard found its way to me. A young woman who lives down the road, Deana, rang me up and told me she had this buzzard in her washing basket. She'd seen it by the side of the road as she'd driven by and because it hadn't flown she'd known something was wrong. She'd reversed back to have a look. The buzzard wasn't moving. It was stunned.

This was a main road and she had a child in the car, so it was dangerous, but she got out, took a coat and used it to scoop up the buzzard and bring it back to the car. Again – with its sharp talons – there was a danger of something going wrong, with the child right there. But she got it home and made a nest for it in the washing basket. She'd been about to call the vet but then she remembered that I was just up the road, and she called me. I went down to see.

This buzzard leaned to the left and was plainly dazed – it had probably been hit by a car. But it didn't seem badly hurt, just in shock. I took it to the vet in South Molton and he didn't think anything was broken; there was no surgery required. What the buzzard needed was time to recover. I took it home, and Julie went out and bought some minced meat. I had to have a cage, and the vet had specified it had to be quite a small one to begin with, because he shouldn't be able to open his wings, he should keep as still as possible, so he'd be rested.

I put him in his cage in my office. To begin with he wouldn't eat; he was too shocked. I thought maybe he wasn't keen on mince, so I went out to get him some roadkill. As luck would have it, I drove round and got three pheasants for him. I stripped out the breast meat, and at last he ate something. This was the first sign we'd had that he might get better. We called him Tommy.

Of course, a buzzard doesn't eat that often, I had to remember that. We tried to give him a bit of variety in his diet. Over the road live Lynda and Justin and their two children, Jodie and Milly, aged five and six or so. Jodie came and told me they had a mouse in their pantry and they were going to set a trap. If they caught the mouse, did Tommy want to eat it? Certainly, I said. The next day there was big news: the mouse was dead in the trap. I went over there and found Lynda too frightened to fetch it out from under the sink. But little Jodie, brave as could be, went in under there and pulled it out and proudly handed it to me. We took it over to my office and tempted Tommy with it, but it didn't look like he was going to take it. Then I remembered that I should be filming this and I turned round, just for two seconds, to switch on the camera. By the time I'd turned back – *woof!* – The mouse had gone.

Tommy was getting better.

Johnny Dollimore rang and said, 'I got a rabbit for Tommy.' It seemed like the whole village was helping keep this buzzard. The rabbit went down, fur and all. A bird like that needs to eat fur and feathers as well as the meat; it's how his system works.

Tommy needed a bigger cage now, so that he could open his wings a bit. I bought the next cage for £5 in South Molton market. A fortnight later he needed a bigger one still. My son Craig provided that one, a parrot cage he happened to have. Then I started to open the door a bit, so Tommy could come out and sit in the office with me. He made a hell of a mess. He squirted over everything in there – the settee, the shelves, the computer, everything. And the smell was awful. But when he flew out the cage and settled up on the pair of royal stag antlers I've got up on the wall, and spread his huge wings out as wide as they'd go – that was a beautiful sight, and I could tell he was going to recover. Also in my office, as it happens, is a stuffed buzzard. I'd found it, dead, caught by a car on the North Devon link road – and I'd had it stuffed. I now have this wonderful picture of Tommy, the live buzzard, face to face with the stuffed one. They're staring at one another. The next thing Tommy did was to head straight back to his cage, as if to say, 'Get me out of here, look what happens to buzzards round here . . .'

It was a sad day when it was time to let Tommy go. A

whole gang of us – Julie, Janet, Dave and Jenni Gale, John Dollimore, Deana and Ian, Darryl, the kids, Craig – were out there standing in the middle of the field. There was a mist sitting on the ground, and a soft quietness that comes with that kind of morning. Our voices carried a long way. I put Tommy's cage down, and his audience gathered round. I opened the door. After a moment's hesitation, he was off . . .

He went and perched in a nearby oak tree and looked back at us. He shook out his feathers – I suppose he was saying, 'Thank God that's over,' and then he flew to the next tree. Now that he knew his wings were working again, he was gone, he disappeared into the fog.

Of course there are some creatures that have still eluded me. I'd love to get a picture of the Beast of Exmoor.

I've tried. Seventeen years ago Eric and Ruth up at Drewstone Farm lost a large number of lambs and sheep. Some had their ears torn off and were killed in such a way that indicated it was a big cat that had done it. Eric and Ruth had heard a fearful screaming sound that they could only imagine was the Beast. They got hold of all the farmers in the area who had guns, and me and my mate were included because we had rifles and a licence to use them. They also called in the Royal Marines, who agreed to help in the search for the Beast. This went on for a while. One or two stray dogs got shot. A mate and I were posted on the railway line, around midnight. This was at the bottom of a long steep, wooded valley, in pitch darkness, so it was like being in a tunnel. We were ghostified enough already, without anything happening. We stood together, waiting, till around two in the morning, when this awful, high-pitched screaming split the air. It chilled the blood. It shivered right through both of us. We jumped in the truck straight away, peering through the darkness to see what we could see.

Nothing. But I've no doubt that's what we heard. Nothing else could have made such an unearthly, piercing sound, not so loud as that.

Years later, my wife Julie and son Craig were driving along the North Devon link road when they saw a big black cat. There was no question in their minds that it was a puma or suchlike. And on another occasion seven of us were down in the Barle valley and saw a big cat two or three hundred yards away, bouncing through the grass, left to right, chasing two deer. But I didn't catch it on film and that's what would prove it beyond a doubt. Some of the hunting people say that if there is a beast, then the hounds would put it up, but of course a cat can climb a tree in a second and the hounds would just go on by and not know any different. I'm sure that thing is out there. I heard that same screaming sound again up at

Twitchen, four years ago. A photograph or piece of film would settle it. I hope it's me that gets it.

In September 1996 Father was taken into hospital in Barnstaple. He'd struggled against cancer before, but it had come back and got him. You could see it – a swelling like a tyre around his middle, which was slowly creeping upwards, getting bigger. He was eighty-five years old, a small man but tough as nails. Nobody pushed him around and if they tried to, they were in trouble.

The cancer was moving closer to his heart and there was nothing anyone could do. He was moved to a private room. There was no doubt, he was dying. He had his wife and children in the room. He couldn't talk, but he looked at us and he lifted his finger and counted, his finger moving from one to the next, to the next. His lips moved, but without any sound. I think he wanted to check we were all there, all present and correct. But there were two girls missing: my sister Julie, and my wife Julie.

I will never forget that, the way he pointed at us, one after the other. It seemed like more than words could say. He was very ill. The band of cancer around his middle moved higher; it reached his heart.

In the end, he drowned – technically speaking. His lungs couldn't cope with the amount of fluid. I held his hand and prayed silently, 'Please take my dad. Please take my dad.' It was awful to watch his suffering, his weakening. All he'd taught us, all he'd given to me and my sisters, suddenly seemed to be slipping away. And yet I wanted him to be gone. It was his time. It was terrible, this illness. I prayed, 'Please take my dad.'

And, of course, he was taken; he died. I held his hand all the while.

I had such a store of memories of him. He'd loved playing skittles. He'd loved his garden – growing gooseberries as big as golfballs and parsnips three feet long . . . he'd made sure there was always food on the table. At work in the quarry – the Powder Monkey, the Cat. On the banks of the river, with a West of England sack full of fish. Walking over the fields with that .410 over his arm. In the lane, showing me the cuckoo's nest. The overalls, with the tobacco and the snuff in the bib pocket.

He'd wanted to be cremated, and so he was. There was a plan to bury his remains in the rose garden in the hospital grounds, where they had been so kind to him and spent so many hours looking after him. But I'd shared such a lot of time with father in graveyards, and I set my heart on putting him into the ground myself. Mother agreed it should happen like that.

He'd lived within spitting distance of the church at High Bray and he'd dug many graves there. Some of those we'd done together. He'd always said to me, 'Don't put me up that end, will you?' And he'd pointed to the top of the churchyard. It was colder, less sunny, up there, and it felt a bit deserted because the path to the entrance of the church didn't pass by. The bottom half was a more sociable place. People walked past on their way to attend services. The sun caught it for most of the day.

And of course there was one particular corner that he'd walked across himself, with me for eleven years and on his own for over fifty – on his way to work. It was the corner where his grandson, Paul, was buried, the little boy who'd died of a brain tumour and whom Father had nursed in such tragic circumstances. Should he, then, share little Paul's grave? My sister Shirley and her husband Derek – Paul's parents – agreed that was best.

We had a little coffin made for Father's remains, with a brass plaque on it. It brought to mind the child's coffin he himself had carried through the snow for three miles – his own firstborn. And Paul's coffin, which he'd seen into the earth, his own grandson. A second grandson – Thelma's son Matthew – had also died, aged eight. All these thoughts jostled in my mind as I dug in that same spot that had been lifted before, by Uncle Arthur, for little Paul's funeral. It was a hard task, to turn each spadeful of this earth that Father had trodden each working day, for so long. It hurts even now to remember it. When I'd finished, and I leaned on the shovel to rest, I could see over the bank, down the hill and across the river, to where the quarry was cutting into the hill on the other side – the quarry where he'd worked, the only job he'd ever had, a lifetime's work, sixty years, showing now as a grey shadow seen through trees. The machines were quiet that day. It was a Saturday; no one was there. Most of the men had gone to the cremation service. The burial of the Powder Monkey's ashes would be attended only by close family.

So we buried him in the same grave as his grandson, Paul. He was a believer, my father, although he didn't go to church because he thought it was hypocritical to attend a place of worship and go to the pub on the same day. None the less, he was a believer. I hope he was looking down on us as we stood in a circle around that small grave. I like to picture him, moving his finger, counting us.

We were all there. We all miss him.

Just over ten years ago, a man called David Parker contacted me and asked if he might use some of my footage for a programme he was making for HTV. I'm not sure to this day how he heard about me – perhaps he'd seen *The Secret of Happiness* or one of the other times I'd been on television. In any case, that's how it started. He bought some shots from my archive for use in his programmes.

I have been working with their production company, Available Light, ever since. David Parker and his wife Wendy McLean not only took me up, they pushed me on, brought more opportunities my way. As I write this, we have all just been to Lapland, making a film with the BBC, and I was laughing at Wendy's ringtone on her mobile phone, which was put there by her son Tom. Instead of the phone ringing his voice says 'Pick up the phone,' over and over. And the relationship between myself and them has brought me to where I am now. It has been so valuable and I want to thank them for their continued support and belief in me.

As I said, it started with just a few sequences from my archive that David bought for HTV. There was very little money involved. Then it took a step up – a fifteen-minute slot for *Wild Westcountry,* and that kind of thing. We made a film called *The Year of the Deer.* We started to bed down together. Wildlife programmes for the BBC are commissioned out of BBC Bristol, and we found ourselves going up there for various awards that we'd been put up for. We never won, but we came close. It wasn't the same as *The Secret of Happiness,* which had had such a big effect that we'd spent weeks in our front room answering phones and filling envelopes – that experience was like being picked up and then dropped again. This started smaller, but it grew. It put my name on the map. One of the times I went up to Bristol I met

David Attenborough – that was such a grand moment. I was learning my craft, making my way.

I made a film called *This Land* for BBC Wales, and that was half an hour on my own. This time, it felt like I was climbing the ladder properly. It felt like I wasn't going to fall off.

All my life I've stalked deer, first with a rifle and then with a camera. The most important thing to take into account is the wind direction. If the wind is blowing towards you, they won't catch your scent. The next most important thing is camouflage. I'm lucky enough to have been sponsored for the last year by a clothing company called the Real Tree. They are brilliant. I can kit myself out top to toe in exactly the right gear, including gloves and mask.

I have a lifetime's experience of where the deer are on Exmoor, but I still use the same tricks as any other stalker. I look at their tracks, which point you in the right direction and a lot more besides. If you can judge how fresh the footprints are, it gives you a rough idea of how far away the deer might be. The size of the tracks is a description of the deer itself – if you split your two fingers in a V-shape and make the V as wide as possible, a track matching that shape will be that of a full-sized male. A narrower V is a hind. The smallest of all is a calf.

I knew, this time, that I might be lucky if I stayed right where I was, on the side of a wooded valley. The wind was towards me. I could hear a big stag roaring further down, and it was getting closer. The best I could do was conceal myself and wait. The trunk of an old fallen tree lay nearby, and I put myself in position, lying down and merging with this tree as much as possible. I had time to work this out so every inch of me was undistinguishable from my surroundings. I waited, and listened to that stag's roar coming closer.

First to appear was a hind. It was quite windy and she was jumpy, but she didn't have a clue I was there. She came on towards me. Other hinds and yearlings followed. And then came the stag, a four and three-a-top, very widely spread – a fine head, very impressive. I lay there, and that stag came within 10 yards of me. He roared right down the camera lens. It was incredible. I could have reached out and touched him. In the end there were thirty hinds and six stags. For one and a half hours I filmed them.

Eventually a hind came round the other side of my tree. Now she was downwind of me. She caught my scent and immediately started to bark and trot away. The next moment the herd were in flight. They were gone. I was exhausted but elated – it had been some of my best filming of stags and hinds.

It is dangerous being near a big male stag in the rutting season. There are times when I've been lucky to escape injury. I'd been tracking this big black stag for three days – following his deep, rich voice through the Ringcombe valley. I had a lad with me on this occasion, also called Johnny, and he waited up in an oak tree. I ended up behind a big round bale of hay in the field atop the valley and this stag knew I was there. He struck the ground with his front feet, and he wiped the earth with his antlers, tossing sprays of grass into the air. He was ready to be very nasty indeed, and those points were sharp. He'd go for me, no mercy. I was poking my nose out so that I could film him. He decided to let me off this time and I followed him further down the valley. We came near a pheasant pen – a fenced enclosure for breeding pheasants. On the other side of this pen the ground fell away into the wood, down to the river. Two or three hinds passed, then two more. Suddenly the big stag jumped out over the fence, only yards away. At first he roared facing away, then he turned and squared up to me. He swung his head and roared again. He was wondering what that thing was with the mask on. The camera was rolling all this time. I was cornered – the fence was at my back. There was no way I was going anywhere. He roared again and walked towards me. I thought Id had it. He was now about six yards from me and roared straight at the camera. At the last moment he slid off to one side and jumped the fence. I was saved. Christ, that was close; he went past only yards away. Gradually he went off into the cover and took his hinds with him. I'd been scared stiff.

My wife Julie has come stalking deer with me, too. She's had the thrill of big stags passing close by while we lay hidden. It was in summertime, when the stags' antlers were covered in velvet. I never tire of getting as close as I can to the wildlife here and bringing it home, to put on films to show people. I was getting better at it, more experienced with the camera and the narration, and as my confidence grew, more opportunities came my way.

I was pleased as Punch when Lesley Bull, from down at the Black Cock, wrote a song about me which Dave Gale set to music. They called it 'The Ballad of Johnny Kingdom'. Here are a couple of the verses:

There's a nature-loving person
To the north of Bishop's Nym
Who thinks he's studying wildlife;
Actually they're studying him.

He crawls around for hours
In all weathers, wind and rain,
Invisible, he thinks, but they say
Look he's back again.

Mother and Father together again

" . . . memories of Mother and Father and our life together crowded me. **"**

On 16 September 2003 Mother had to go into hospital for an X-ray as part of her check-up for her cancer treatment which she'd been undergoing for a good few months. Two of my sisters were taking her in. There was no immediate danger, but somehow I felt uncomfortable. I hurried. But why the rush, today, I asked myself. Of course we were all anxious, but . . .

I can't quite say what it was that told me to run on over there. Something else entered the equation – this was urgent, a voice told me.

I drove to the hospital as fast as I could. I parked and hurried into the foyer. Leading away from the entrance hall is a very long corridor, helluva long, and dark. Way down the end of this corridor I could make out two women pushing a wheelchair, away from me. I recognized my sisters; they were taking Mother to the X-ray room. It struck me – the sight of those two distant figures walking away, the wheelchair, the dark corridor – that this was the tunnel of no return and Mother was almost at the end. I called out and they stopped and waited for me. As I walked towards them, the hair stood up on the back of my neck, I don't know why. I caught up with them and we all carried on together.

After the X-ray was completed we went back outside, Mother in her wheelchair. In the foyer we stopped to say our goodbyes. I thought I had let my worries get the better of me. I leaned over to kiss Mother on the cheek. 'See you soon,' I said.

The next day I was stalking up at Stoke Pero. It's a beautiful valley and it was a perfect autumn day. The tracks of the deer were in front of me, the camera was to hand, but I found I couldn't concentrate. My worries returned again and again. A voice nagged at me – go on up to the top of the ridge, don't stay down here where there's no signal on the phone. My footsteps veered uphill. I found myself looking at the signal bars on my phone. As I reached the top, all three bars appeared. The next instant the phone rang. It was Julie, who'd been trying to get hold of me to say that Mother was bad. Could I come quickly?

In fact, Mother had passed away peacefully during the night, but Julie hadn't wanted to tell me, not while I was on my own in the middle of nowhere. I drove straight away to Mother's house in Broomhill Villas, in Brayford, only a stone's throw from where we'd all been brought up in High Bray. Everyone was there already –

my sisters, Julie, our family, our crowd. I was too late to have been with Mother when she'd died, and my heart went out to my sister Thelma, who'd done so much caring for her and who had been the one to find her that morning.

Suddenly I was glad I'd gone to the hospital the day before, that I'd kissed her goodbye and said, 'See you soon.' That dark tunnel – she'd reached the end, and her disappearance was like a closed door.

Julie and I have reached the age, now, where it's not so long until we face that door ourselves. We're young enough and fit and well, but there is something about not having your parents up ahead of you that brings you to realize it's your turn in the queue. Julie's dad had died some years before, and not long after, in 2004, her mum died on the day before Julie's birthday. Julie had promised her mum that she'd never be sent into a hospital, she'd be looked after in the home just at the top of our road, and so she was. And in fact, something odd happened a few days after she died. I was sitting out on the steps in our back garden and a bird pitched right next to me. It looked like a fledgling robin. I was startled it had come so close, and from there it took off and alighted in Julie's mother's shrub, a camellia that had been moved from her garden when she'd gone into the home. Julie came over and looked into the bush to see this bird, and it didn't move, it didn't want to fly away.

She went and made tea and came back out, and the bird flew over and wouldn't leave Julie alone. It went under her feet, it perched on the arm of her seat . . . It was like it was trying to tell her something. It came on to the table and perched on the rim of my mug. Julie called me over to see this, and to have my tea. I saw it there on the mug, just as it flew off into the privet hedge. 'I'd love to have had a picture of that,' I said. I went to fetch my camera in case this extraordinary little bird did anything else. Once I had the camera I called out to the robin, 'Come back, then, and pitch on that cup again for me, will you?' And it did, it came right back and sat on the mug, and I took the picture you can see on this page. No wonder we had the idea that that little bird carried the spirit of Julie's mother, Doris. She was so full of fun.

I've had so many dealings with death over the course of my lifetime that I can look it square in the eye and keep it off for a good many years yet, I hope, with a good joke and a drink and with the help of our friends, my work and our grandchildren to watch growing up. Recently, in fact, I've given up the gravedigging – and believe it or not the last one I dug was my own. I had booked a spot in the cemetery in Bishop's Nympton for Julie and me. It's just a little ways down from where Joe Drewer lies, and I thought it would be fitting to dig it myself. I asked Mike Warren to help, and my son Stuart, who wasn't so keen at the idea, but he agreed. We hired a compressor and jack hammer for the hard, stony ground. It did feel strange to be alive and well, digging away in the pit where I knew I'd end up when my turn came, making jokes with my elder son and my best friend, Mike Warren. 'Poor old Johnny,' Mike would say, 'isn't it a shame he's gone?' When we'd finished Mike said, 'There's one thing wrong.'

'What's that?'

'There's no flowers.'

We filled it back in with soft earth, so I've left an easy job for whichever mechanical digger has to do it when the time comes.

Gravedigging has been a tradition of the Kingdom family for four generations – my grandfather, my father, me and my sons. This rather comical event – a Kingdom man digging his own grave – seemed like a fitting end to that tradition.

Mother had died peacefully in her sleep, and we'd promised that she'd rest alongside Father. We had the same little coffin made as Father's, with a brass plate to match. I returned to the corner of the graveyard with my spade, pick and shovel. It was going to be very hard. I prayed to have the strength to do it. I took a breath and started. With each strike of the pick, with every shovelful of earth I took out, memories of Mother and Father and our life together crowded me. The rattle she'd made for me out of nails. The washing. The ironing. The drawing of water. The care for her six children. That pinafore, with the packet of Player's Weights coming out, lighting up. She had reached the age of eighty-six, near enough the same as Father, so you could say they'd had their fair share of years.

I dug down and reached Father's coffin. What a terrible sorrow took hold of me as I lifted him out. So often he and I had had earth on our hands when we were burying other men and women, the work of many a long year. This was a sad day, without doubt, Mother and Father both gone.

I picked up the spade, pick and shovel, and made the space for them to lie together, just as they had done all their married lives.

In 2004 David Parker of Available Light Productions put together a compilation of clips from programmes we've made together to show Richard Klein, the Commissioning Editor for Documentaries at the BBC. Richard Klein liked what he saw and commissioned eight half-hour programmes to be broadcast nationally on BBC2.

This was a huge step up for me. Instead of bits and pieces within other programmes, or a half-hour programme broadcast just in one particular area of the country, this was to be a whole autumn season of

programmes broadcast on a national channel. We would have a whole year to film the series, so we could cover the animals from winter, through spring and summer, to autumn. I was excited. There was proper money, and a full crew – cameraman, producer, sound, the lot. It was going to be a hell of a year.

I would follow red deer, of course, and badgers are what I'm best known for. But – quite right, too – deer and badgers and Exmoor ponies are on any amount of postcards. We also wanted to film some of the more unusual Exmoor wildlife, the stuff you rarely see.

Slow worms and lizards aren't on any postcards, but they can be found, especially just as they come out of hibernation. And on moorland during April and May you have to be careful not to stumble on a viper. They'll jump at you, vipers will, especially when they're a bit dozy, having just woken from the winter. But your dog has to be more careful. It's far more often that a dog is bitten than a human.

I'm scared of snakes, but the older I get the more I admire them.

As part of the BBC2 series, Shaun and Steve Govier and I went looking for snakes up at Barbrook, near Lynmouth. You could see right over the Bristol Channel towards Wales. It was early April and already very hot. Snakes like fir plantations, because fir roots spread out on the surface of the ground and create soft, well-cushioned hollows underneath them. They like their comfort.

We knew where to go, because the viper, if possible, will go back to the same place to hibernate. When we got to our spot, underneath an old oak tree, last year's leaves were a thick carpet all around, and as we watched and waited, we saw that in one particular place the leaves were moving. The snakes were seething underneath. It sent shivers up your spine. We found one that we could film, and we were four to six feet away. This was dangerously close. You not only have to keep a close eye on the snake in front, but you have to remember they are inquisitive and canny creatures; if you're looking at one, then its mate is not far away, and more than likely it is sneaking round to have a look at you from behind. They won't hurt you if they can avoid it, though.

With more patience, and waiting, we saw a pair of males dancing. They stood up on their tails and wrapped their bodies around each other, swaying back and forth. They stood two feet tall – which is the longest you'll see a viper, although there are quite a few books that will tell you they grow to only 18 inches. It's called 'dancing', but this isn't what's really going on. What they're up to, of course, is fighting. They won't hurt each other, but the males test their dominance over one another in this way to sort out the boundaries to their territory. We also got footage of the snakes mating. The female is brownish in colour, the male is darker, with the zigzag down his back. The film we got was in among the brambles, and a female adder no more than three feet away is looking straight into the barrel of the camera; she unlocks her jaw and opens her mouth – wider than you'd believe. This is a mouth that can swallow a mouse or a frog whole. The sight of it's enough to make you break out in a cold sweat.

This reminds me of a time years ago when me and my dad and a mate were walking the riverbank and we came across a viper. Father stopped us. 'Hold on,' he said, 'take a look at this. Watch.' He eyeballed the snake and walked straight towards it. Behind it was the river; there was no escape. The viper turned, jumped into the river and swam to the other side. We couldn't believe it. They swim.

You do have to be careful, though. I was with Keith Setherton when I saw a viper with his tail well stuck in the ground, ready to jump. I'd no sooner turned to Keith and said, 'Hey, look at that one . . .' when out of the corner of my eye I saw the viper leap three feet in the air towards us.

We also have the non-venomous grass snake in this country. They are a greenish colour and bigger than vipers – but they were not believed to grow as long as six feet, as some people had suggested. I received a telephone call from a cottage near Whitechapel Manor – apparently there was a grass snake six feet long living under the patio. I didn't believe it; I thought it must be an exaggeration. I went up there and waited. I saw nothing. I went up there and waited again. You will understand that the patio of this cottage wasn't the most difficult place to wait, compared with what I usually had to put up with. It was quite comfortable and civilized.

I spent a whole week trying different ways not to alert this grass snake to my presence. When a snake puts its tongue out, it's testing the air for scent, and that tongue is an incredibly delicate instrument. It was only when I made an approach to the house from a totally different direction that I managed to avoid it finding me out. I saw it eventually, and, yes, it was six feet long; there seemed to be an endless length of it coming out from under the patio. It turned out that there was a pond nearby with a plague of frogs in it, and the grass snake had grown so big eating all these frogs. God knows how many it had got through to grow so big. Hundreds. It was so huge, this grass snake, that it looked like it had crocodile skin.

The other unusual animal we were looking to capture on film for the television series was the hare. I can't think of hares without remembering Jim and June Catsby. They bought my granny's house at Bray Cross, and then after that they moved to Bishop's Nympton. Very often I'd go out on the moors with Jim – he was a big strong man, over six feet tall, and he liked to take his Bassett hound out and follow the beagle hunt, on foot, which is the hunt that goes out chasing hares. He was very fit, but in his later years he'd become short of breath. 'Hold on, Johnny,' he'd say, and he'd turn away from me and take a tin out of his pocket, unclip the lid and take out a syringe and inject himself in the stomach. Moments later he'd carry on, right as rain, fitter than I was – I'd need to run to keep up. Jim sadly died last September, leaving June behind, and may he rest in peace. I shall remember all those times we went up on the moor with his Bassett hound.

A hare is a lot bigger than a rabbit, and it's a lot faster with those big back legs pushing it along. It is a gingery colour as opposed to the mink-brown colour of a rabbit, and it has much longer ears with black tips. And it doesn't have a burrow – it lives above ground. I've filmed them boxing – it's the males who stand up and fight like that, getting up on their hind legs and boxing very quickly, a couple of combinations just as if Father had taught them. But it's over so quick; blink and you miss it. I've filmed hares boxing up at Broomhill Farm, near King's Nympton. Graham Clemence has always had hares up there; he doesn't allow any shooting of them. And I was with Julie and our granddaughter once, on the way to the badger hide, when I caught a leveret – a baby hare – in my hands. That was a thrill. They are so fast; to hold one is a rare experience.

I stalked hares with Richard Taylor-Jones for an HTV programme, but we ended up getting involved with an animal about as different from a hare as you could possibly get. With Graham's permission, Richard and I went up to Broomhill Farm to see what we could see. Two hundred yards down the slope was a brown spot. 'What's that?' I said and pointed. Through the glasses we could see it was a hare. But how to approach without it seeing us? We decided to make a left-handed loop along the side of this cleave.

Slowly and patiently we made our way, keeping out of sight of the hare down below. We were as high up the slope as we could be, while making sure we didn't break the skyline. If we did, the hare would spot the movement straight away. Of course, we were focused on the hare beneath us, so when this huge *ROARRR!* came from above we jumped out of our skins. We looked up and saw that this row of cows' heads had suddenly appeared on the horizon, like the Indians were coming. But that roar didn't sound like it had been made by a cow. No way.

Sure enough, bang in the middle of all these cows peering over the top of the hill was a huge bull. He was looking down on us. His wives were strung out on either side of him and he was wondering what we were up to. He didn't like the look of me. I was masked up, on the ground, so no doubt I looked suspicious. I was up to no good. He came closer and bellowed. He pawed the ground. Don't move, I said to myself. It was hard not to, but if I took off down that slope he'd be after me and I'd be done for.

The bull came closer. He roared and stamped his foot. This was serious. He was five feet away. I'd never been in such danger. He was frothing at the mouth and tossing his head and roaring. There was no doubt he was about to charge. Richard saw I was frightened, because I slowly moved a yard backwards, I couldn't help it. The bull came closer. He wasn't going to leave us alone. What to do?

Maybe it was the mask. He didn't like it. He couldn't see what kind of animal I was. Very slowly I got up on my knees. He roared like hell and stamped and frothed at the mouth. I lifted my hand, took hold of the bottom of the mask and drew it up off my face – all dead slow. The bull looked at me. He roared again, but not quite so loud. He turned round. His next roar was quieter again, and then he moved towards the backside of a cow and sniffed it.

The danger was past. He'd worked out I wasn't a threat to him, and at the same time he'd caught the scent of a cow in season, and the two things together meant he was no longer concerned with me. We'd got away with it, we were safe. I nearly . . . Well, we were both frightened to death.

A couple of months later I got a call from Graham. 'Johnny,' he said, 'I thought you ought to know, Malcolm's dead.'

'Who?'

'Your friend Malcolm's upped and died.'

'Who's Malcolm?'

'Malcolm the bull. I thought I should tell you the sad news that he died.'

When they'd taken Malcolm away, he turned out to be over a ton in weight. I still break into a sweat when I think of him stamping and bellowing right over me like that – and thank my lucky stars he didn't get me.

A couple of years ago I was selling my videos in Tiverton market when I fell into conversation with Edna and Mervin Cowling, a couple who were interested in wildlife. They owned a stretch of woodland near Bishop's Nympton, where I live. The conversation turned to the subject of badgers. 'You like badgers?' they asked, and I replied, 'Yes, I do.' They told me of the badger sett in their woods and they invited me to go and film there, if I wanted to.

A while later I took a lad who works over the road, Darryl Turner, who's fourteen, and we went to see what we could see. It was spring, and these woods were a

336   **JOHNNY KINGDOM**

carpet of bluebells. We found the badger sett and we sat down beside an oak tree some distance downwind. In the middle of the bluebells, with the late evening sun slanting down through an oak tree above us, it was like being in heaven.

Darryl and I waited for two hours, and then our patience paid off. Two badgers came out, and then the sow, the female badger, was followed out by three small cubs, only eight to ten inches long. And the cubs began to play, rolling around together and standing up on their hind legs, pushing and wrestling and tumbling on the ground. These magical creatures were unaware of our presence and, like always, it was a God-given privilege to observe them.

The next time, I went with my second cameraman for the BBC2 series, Rupert Smith. We filmed five badgers playing. One nearly came close enough to touch.

Edna and Mervin Cowling owned this lovely piece of woodland for their own pleasure, and had no intention of developing it or building on it, apart from the track they made so they could get around it on the quad bike.

I asked if I could build a hide, and they said yes. It fitted in with what they wanted for their land – a place for wildlife, and for people to see wildlife. It also suited the purposes of the BBC2 series. They could film us building the hide and with their contribution from the budget we could make a better job of it.

In September 2005 Jamie Stoneman of North Devon Scaffolding turned up with twelve men and we set to work. I can't say how much it meant to me to have so much help given to me so generously. Jonathan Becklake loaned me a tractor and trailer. By now, of course, I had some experience of building hides and I'd progressed from leaky, tatty old things that moved around in the wind to strong, well-camouflaged, weathertight and comfortable structures.

We went up 29 feet high with this new hide, and we bought a ten by eight foot shed and hauled it up there on to the platform in sections. Mike Warren and I watched from the bottom as the hut was screwed together, the insulation fitted, and shutters cut in the sides. Bird boxes were countersunk into it, too, with cameras set permanently into each one. My nephew Simon Carter was chippie for us. The whole thing was done in two days. Then it was time for camouflage – and Paul from Real Tree clothing was a great help. We used seventy-five rolls of duck tape to hide the scaffold bars. We also put a line up to hang the bird feeders on, but of course the squirrels were first on the scene, running along the wire and attacking the feeders, but they quickly learned it was better to gnaw through the wire – steel wire, mind – and drop the whole thing on the bloody floor. They're clever devils, squirrels, and wherever there are bird feeders there are squirrels stealing the food. The sparrowhawk is also tempted to come along, because he loves a small bird to eat – cruel, but that's nature.

This new hide is wonderful. At the time of writing it is again May, and the bluebells are back, and I can sit in comfort up in my little house in the trees and watch this year's badger cubs come out and play.

Halfway through the filming of the series David Parker brought Richard Klein, the BBC2 commissioning editor, and his daughter down here to visit – and the idea was for us all to go out and see what we could see. They came to my house in Bishop's Nympton, and when Richard came in first, his little daughter Ellen was very shy of me and wouldn't talk. She was frightened even to look at me.

We went outside and climbed in the truck. Richard Klein fetched out the kiddy seat from his own car and he fixed it in the front passenger seat. Ellen was my companion now. She had the best view. We went up to Twitchen, on the moor, and quite soon we saw thirty-odd deer. It's not so difficult, if you know where to go, to see deer from far off; the difficulty is to get at all close. I asked little Ellen if she wanted to see them close up, and she nodded. We all set off on foot and it wasn't the best weather. We got soaking wet and it was quite a way. She soldiered on, brave as anything. Eventually we did get close to the deer, and she saw everything. When we got back to the vehicle her father had a change of clothes for her. We went on to Tarr Steps and saw the Exmoor ponies. In the afternoon we went to see the new badger hide we'd made in the Cowlings' woods.

By the end of the day Ellen was holding my hand and she wasn't the least bit scared of me. Her father Richard Klein had given our lives such a leg up, it was a wonderful feeling to share a nice day out with him and his daughter.

During the day Richard had told David Parker and myself that he'd liked what he'd seen of the filming we'd done so far. He said he wanted to give us ten programmes instead of eight.

This has been an extraordinary year for our family. I've been working hard. I have a schedule like you wouldn't believe. This isn't the Johnny Kingdom of yesteryear. I have to attend meetings, I flew to Lapland twice to make a TV Christmas special, I went by train to Bristol to attend a publishing meeting in a hotel. My shotguns and rifles are gathering dust while I deal with production budgets and proof pages and God knows what else. I no longer carry a fox-wire with me at all times.

It's difficult to hold all the strands of my life together,

and remember back to the boy who kept mice and skinned moles, who pulled trout out of the river, who fell through the garage roof, who sleepwalked around the house and chased girls into cupboards. All I know is that I've had the best out of what life has to offer. And so much of that is to do with animals. But we are all God's creatures, and our best satisfactions and pleasures are to be found as close to the ground as we can get. I hope and trust there are more to come. I know there are, I can feel it in my bones.

Ten minutes ago, something happened that fills me with such pleasure that I can hardly put it down quick enough. I received a telephone call from Mervin Cowling, the owner of the woodland where I built my new hide.

Their kind offer is that Julie and I should buy that twenty acres of woodland from them. They'd always thought, apparently, that they'd sell it to us eventually, but they decided to bring their decision forward.

That hide I've built – it will never have to come down. There is no one who can chase me off, no one can come along and say, Johnny, I'm sorry, you have to take that down now and move on. I will have a bluebell wood of my own.

It is a wonderful feeling, it's kind of like coming home. The land is bigger and better than I could ever have imagined owning. Now I will be able to walk those acres; and every tree and bramble and blade of grass is growing – and all its creatures are breeding and feeding and fighting – on my patch, and that is my pleasure. I am never shy of receiving pats on the back, congratulations of any type are always welcome, it's true, but it feels like the biggest and best 'well done', to have fate, or to have God's hand, or whatever it is, take such a turn as to bring this to our family, here, now.

I want to thank the Cowlings from the bottom of my heart. My family will enjoy their land and keep it safe and well. I wish them both a good retirement – Mervin and Edna, God bless you, from Johnny Kingdom and his family.

I will continue to make wildlife programmes, I hope. And I'm proud at how such programmes have become a major force in the world of conservation. We can see – as never before – the riches that we possess in the variety and beauty of the wildlife that is all around. We can lift up a brick in our back yard and see it, or we can find it in a spider's web in the corner of the bathroom. On television, the most extraordinary of nature's designs are brought to us in our living rooms, whether we live in the middle of a big city or in the middle of nowhere. And – when we can see it, we learn to care about it. And if we care about it, we seek to preserve it.

Shortly before she died, Mother said to me, 'You will

reach the top.' With this feeling in my heart, and looking out from the top pasture above my woodland over to where I was born and where she raised us – just a mile or two away – I can tell her now, 'Yes I did. Look.'

INDEX

PICTURE CREDITS

Background page 10–11; main pictures pages 20, 22–3, 26–7, 28–9, 30–1, 32 © Richard Taylor Jones.

All other pictures courtesy Johnny Kingdom.

ACKNOWLEDGEMENTS

There are so many people who have helped me in my personal and professional life. Some are mentioned in the book, but I'd like to put all their names here and give them my thanks.

My family: my wife Julie of course, to whom this book is dedicated, and my eldest son Stuart and his wife Sue and their daughter Louise, my second son Craig and his partner Jane, and his daughter Roxy and her mum, Gabrielle. My sisters and their families: Shirley and her family, Julie and Tony and family, Susan and Mike, Rosalind and Martin and family, Thelma and Anthony. And last but not least, my brother-in-law Terry Carter and his family.

Special thanks go to people who've let me build hides on their land: Alan Chesterfield, Clifford Woollacott, Terry Rudd, Tony Thorne, Mervin and Edna Cowling. Also – Steve and Jackie Mason and the Nicholls family.

And the brilliant people who helped me so much in building those hides: my sons, Mike Warren, Pete Webster, Steve Govier, Paul Kingdon and Richard Kingdon, Robert and Jenny Kingdon, Jamie Stoneman and his workmen. Also Frankie Hooper, Richard Jennings, Gary Setherton, Dennis Woollacott, Nicky Hutter, Paul Setherton and my nephew Simon Carter.

And there are those who were very kind in helping to look after Bambi – Justin Simmons and Lynda Warren and their children Jodie and Milly, The late Joe Drewer, of course, and his family Rene and Angela. The late Adrian Adams, his wife Carol and the kids Ryan and Genna. Jill Warren, for the goats' milk. Tony Dean and last but not least, Bambi's vet, Martin Prior.

I'd like to thank those who've helped me produce this book – Christine Zaba, Hilary Knight, Jane Turnbull, Sam North, and the team at Transworld: Doug Young, Emma Musgrave, Alison Barrow and the designer Isobel Gillan. Special thanks for Tony Dean , the Badger Man, for letting me get right up close to the badgers in his sett for the cover photo on the hardback of this book.

During the filming years there are many who've supported me – Dave Parker, Wendy McLean, Mike Warren, James Cutler, Richard Taylor-Jones, Rupert Smith, Mostafa Hammuri, Amanda Reilly, Tony Jones, Graham Clemence, Brian Leatherby, Dick and Simone Williams, Jenny and Barry Bailey, Mr Brierley, Bob Cockram, Fred and Jenny Hayes and family, Sarah Waite, Mike Birch, Julian Bishop, Sid and Mary Payne, Dave Gale, Tony Keene, Lesley Whinslade, Lesley Bull, Mike Fook, Terry Moule, Dennis Hunt, Eric and Ruth Ley and family, Paul Naptin at Real Tree, Dave Barrow, Andrew and Jan Jones, Steve and Jane Westacott, Horace Blackmoor, Alan Walton, Bob and Cheryl Woolcott, John Becklake, Jan and Vic Boorman, Chris and John Dollimore, Jeremy Hutter, Darryl Turner, Ian and Deana Stamate and family, the late Les Greenslade, Gordon and Loraine and family, Jenny and Cliff Ham, Hazel and John Mildon and family, Fran and Dennis Gunn, Steve Bramley. Wallace and Evelyn Pugsley, Henry Saunders, John and Bridget Goscombe from Sindercombe, Bert Kingdon, Peter Chandler, Brian Pugsley, John Blake, Mr and Mrs Holt Stevens of West Molland, Raymond Jones and Dennis Jones, Don Lewis, Keith Ross of Tantivy in Dulverton, Desmond Thorne, Ricky and Mary Werner, Michael and Marlene Jones, The National Trust, Lloyd Ayre, Kingdon's Hardware, Mary, Lesley and Catherine from Southside Stores, Garth and Angela Chanter, Dick Barton the vet, Kelvyn Warren, Raymond Jones and Mr and Mrs Handcock from Hineham. Les and Sally Chilcott and family, the late Bruce Woolaway, Gary Woolaway and family of the Commodore Hotel in Instow (not forgetting Bob the chef).

And the people who've made all the difference – Mike Warren gets yet another mention and his wife Jill, Bob and Jenny Artless, Paul and Margaret Kingdon and their children Robert and Jenni, Brian and Maureen Leatherby, Graham Clemence, Roger and Amanda Gregory, Tony Thorne and finally, Revd Pennington.